The Insider's Pocket Guide to Horse Racing

Also by Jim Bolus

Run for the Roses
Kentucky Derby: The Chance of a Lifetime
(with Joe Hirsch)

The Insider's Pocket Guide to Horse Racing

JIM BOLUS

TAYLOR
PUBLISHING
COMPANY
DALLAS, TEXAS

Published by Taylor Publishing Company
                1550 West Mockingbird Lane
                Dallas, Texas 75235

Designed by David Timmons

Library of Congress Cataloging-in-Publication Data
Bolus, Jim
    The insider's pocket guide to horse racing / Jim Bolus.
            p.   cm.
        ISBN 0-87833-706-7 : $9.95
        1. Horse race betting. 2. Horse-racing. I. Title.
SF331.B57 1990
798.401—dc20
                                                    89-49631
                                                        CIP

Printed in the United States of America
10 9 8 7 6 5 4 3 2 1

To Suzanne, Bo, and Jen

Contents

Acknowledgments

I am indebted to Cathy Schenck and Doris Waren, both from the Keeneland Library, and Theresa Fitzgerald, librarian for *The Blood-Horse* magazine.

I wish to thank trainers Jack Price, Harvey Vanier, Sylvester Veitch, W. C. "Woody" Stephens, Charlie Rose, D. Wayne Lukas, and Cheryl Kolbrick; jockeys Jim McKnight, Pat Day, and Jorge Velasquez; and racing secretary Howard Battle. Also, special thanks go to retired racing steward Keene Daingerfield and to Dr. Manuel A. Gilman, the steward representing The Jockey Club at New York Racing Association tracks.

I also owe thanks to handicappers Don DeWitt and Mike Battaglia, as well as to two longtime friends who have been tremendous help to me through the years, former Louisville newspaperman Mike Barry and Billy Reed, president of the National Turf Writers Association.

In addition, I would like to thank the following racetrack publicity offices for their assistance: Churchill Downs, Keeneland, Turfway Park, the Ontario Jockey Club, Calder Race Course, Philadelphia Park, Ak-Sar-Ben, Arlington International Racecourse, Ladbroke Detroit Race Course, Laurel, Santa Anita Park, and Monmouth Park.

I wish to thank, too, the *Daily Racing Form*, The Jockey Club, and the National Museum of Racing for their assistance.

Publications that were helpful as references were the *Thoroughbred Racing Associations' 1989 Directory & Record Book*, the *1989 New York Racing Association Media Guide*, the *Daily Racing Form*, *The Louisville Times*, various issues of

The Blood-Horse magazine, and various editions of *The American Racing Manual*.

And finally, on a personal note, I wish to thank my entrymate, Suzanne (my wife of 25 years), for her contributions to this book and for her never-ending support.

1

How to Read a Racing Form

THE DAILY RACING FORM

Without the "Bible," you really don't have a prayer at the races.

The "Bible of Racing," that is.

We're talking about the *Daily Racing Form*, and nobody can expect to be a serious handi-capper without it. Known as America's Turf Authority, the *Form* contains the past performances on all of the horses racing on the card, as well as charts of the races and a list of daily workouts.

The *Form* can be intimidating at first glance. What are all those numbers and letters and ab-breviations? What does it all mean?

Well, learning to read the *Form* is a fairly easy assignment . . . so let's go through a step-by-step lesson. First of all, though, it should be noted that the *Form* has different editions. Its Eastern edition is the broadsheet paper in which each past-per-formance line is three columns wide. Two-column past performances are published in the *Form's* tabloid editions printed in Chicago, Los Angeles, Seattle, and Toronto. The past-performance infor-mation in these editions is essentially the same, though printed in a different format.

With that understanding, let's now take a look

at the information that the *Form* provides its readers. Listed for each horse is his owner, trainer, and breeder, as well as his color, sex, breeding (sire, dam, and sire of dam), and the weight that he will carry in this particular race. Also included is his record (starts, firsts, seconds, thirds, and earnings) for both the past 2 years and his lifetime. The horse's record on the turf is also listed.

Mud marks appear alongside the names of those horses that have demonstrated ability on off tracks. An asterisk refers to a fair mud runner, an "x" means the horse is a good mud runner, and an "x" with a circle around it signifies that this horse is a superior mud runner.

The past performances show you how a horse has performed in his most recent starts. Each of these starts contains a line going across the page that provides you with the following information:

- Date of the race
- Number of the race on the card (first, third, etc.)
- The track where the race was run
- The distance of the race
- The fractional times for that race (say, $22^4/5$ seconds for the first quarter, :46 for the half-mile, etc. A note: thoroughbred racing breaks its times down into fifths of a second.)
- Final time of the first horse to finish the race
- The track condition (fast, sloppy, etc.)
- Approximate closing odds: An asterisk preceding the odds means that the horse was the favorite; an "e" following the odds means that the horse was part of an entry, which is two or more horses coupled in the betting; an "f" means that the horse was in the mutuel field, which is made up of the horses who figure to have the smallest chance of winning.
- Weight carried by the horse in this race
- First call: If the horse was third at the first call, 3 lengths behind the leader, the number 3

will appear with another 3—a superior figure—alongside.

• Second call: If the horse was third at this point of the race, now 2 lengths behind the leader, the number 3 will appear with a 2—a superior figure—next to it.

• Stretch call: which is made about an eighth of a mile from the finish If the horse was now second, a length behind the leader, the number 2 will appear with a 1—a superior figure—alongside.

• Finish: If the horse won by a nose, the number 1 will appear with the abbreviation for a nose—"no"—next to it. If the horse was second, beaten by 3 lengths, the number 2 will appear with a 3—a superior figure—alongside.

• Jockey and post position

• Claiming price or type of race (If a circled F appears here, that means that the race was exclusively for fillies or fillies and mares.)

• Speed rating: The speed rating is a comparison of the horse's final time with the best clocking made at that distance at that particular track within the previous 3 calendar years. Speed ratings are figured by subtracting from 100 each fifth of a second that that particular horse's time is slower than the best previous time during the past 3 years. If the best time is $1:07^4/_5$ for 6 furlongs and the horse won this particular race in $1:11^3/_5$, that's $3^4/_5$ seconds off the best time—or 19 fifths. Thus, the speed rating is 81. If the horse ran a $1:07^4/_5$ to equal the best time, the speed rating is 100. If he ran in $1:07^2/_5$, the speed rating is 102, $^2/_5$ faster than the previous best.

• Track Variant: Following the speed rating is the track variant, which is the average number of points (or lengths) faster or slower than the 3-year best time for all horses running on the same program the same day. Under a new formula, separate track variants are figured for races under 1 mile and at 1 mile and over, both on the dirt and on turf.

- First 3 finishers in the race
- Number of starters
- Sped Index: In 1989, the *Form* introduced something new called the speed index, which is figured by adding the speed rating and track variant numbers for the applicable races and comparing their total to the number 100. If a horse has a speed rating of 90 and the track variant is 8, then the total of the two is 98 and the speed index is –2. Four speed index numbers are listed for each horse—the first one for the most recent start at the same conditions for the race he is running, the second showing the average of his last 3 races that fit the conditions of the race he is running, the third showing the average of all starts (up to 12) at the conditions, and the fourth giving an overall average of all starts (up to 12), including all distances and surfaces.
- Workouts: The most recent workouts appear under the past performances for each horse. A bullet (a black dot) alongside a workout means that this was the fastest workout of the day at that track and at that distance. The date, the track, the distance, the track condition, and the time for the workouts are listed, along with a designation as to how the horse worked in each. Those designations are:

     b—breezing
     d—driving
     e—easily
     h—handily
     bo—bore out

In addition, the letter "g" means that the horse worked from the starting gate, and the letter "T" in a circle means that the workout came on the turf course.

The past performances are produced from a chart of a race prepared by a chart caller and a call taker. The chart pinpoints the running position of every horse at designated points during a race. The caller watches the race from the press box, his binoculars trained on the field, and as the race unfolds, he calls out the horses and their positions with the margins, while the call taker writes down the information. Chart callers also have the opportunity to watch the rerun on video tape, which enables them to review the race. Calling races is an art, and the *Form* has some talented chart callers throughout the country.

Abbreviations used in the points of call:

no—nose
hd—head
nk—neck

Racetrack condition abbreviatlons:

Dirt courses	*Grass courses*
ft—fast	hd—hard
gd—good	fm—firm
sl—slow	gd—good
sy—sloppy	yl—yielding
m—muddy	sf—soft
hy—heavy	
fr—frozen	

OW TO READ DAILY RACING FORM PAST PERFORMANCES

ast Performances include cumulative statistics for every horse who has raced on the grass in the U.S. and foreign ountries; a symbol ⑤ pointing out restricted races (not for open company) as well as races for horses bred in a specific ate, and a "bullet" ● denoting superior workouts (the best workout of the day at that track for that distance).

FOREIGN-BRED: An asterisk preceding the horse's name indicates he was bred in a foreign country. The country of origin (abbreviated) appears er the breeder's name, as does the state or place and Canadian province of all horses foaled in the United States, Puerto Rico or Canada.

MUD MARKS: One of the following symbols after a horse's name reflects an expert's opinion of his ability on an off track:

﹡ Fair Mud Runner   ✕ Good Mud Runner   ⊗ Superior Mud Runner

RECORD OF STARTS AND EARNINGS: Each horse's lifetime statistics are given as well as his complete racing record for the current and prior ar, or the last two years in which he competed. The letter M in the current year's record indicates the horse is a maiden. M in the previous year's ord indicates the horse was a maiden at the end of that year. TURF RECORD shows his lifetime starts, wins, seconds, thirds and earnings on the ss.

Horse	Mud Mark	Today's Weight	Color	Sex	Age	Pedigree		Today's Claiming Price		Earnings Record			
			Ch.	f.	4	by Ridan—Miss Hopes, by Jet Pilot							
ood Hopes ﹡			Br. Jones H G (Cal)						1981	12	3	2	1	$20,280
a.—Good Hope Farm	1175	Tr. Jones H G					$12,000	1980	4	M	0	2	$1,100
		Lifetime	20	3	3	4	$23,600		Turf	4	1	0	1	$6,500

un81-6Hol 6f :224 :46 1:113 ft *6-5e 1175 33 32 21 1no SmithT3 ⑫ ⑤ c12000 81 GoodHpes,LionTmr,HppyDys 12
lly 28 Dmr 3f ft :37b   ●Jun 25 Hol 4f ft :46h   ●Jun 30 Hol 3f ft :362h   May 25 Hol 4f ft :49b

NOTE: Latest workouts are printed under each horse's past performances when they are available. The "bullet" ● indicates it was the best workout e day at the track and distance.

The column labels pointing down to the data line (left to right):

- Day
- Month
- Year
- Number of Race
- Track Raced On
- Distance
- Fractional Times of Horse in Lead at Each Of These Points
- Time of Winner
- Track Condition
- Denotes Favorite
- Closing odds
- Coupled in Wagering (entry)
- Weight Carried
- Apprentice Allowance
- First Call
- Second Call
- In Stretch

30Jun81-6Hol 6f :22⁴ :46 1:11³ ft *6-5e 1175 33 32 21

EVERYTHING YOU WAN

30Jun81- 6Hol 6f :22⁴ :46 1:11³ ft *6-5e 1175 33 32 21
DATE RACE WAS RUN The day, month and year. This race was on

30Jun81-**6Hol** 6f :22⁴ :46 1:11³ ft *6-5e 1175 33 32 21
NUMBER OF RACE AND TRACK RACED ON This was the sixth race
for a complete list of track abbreviations. The ♦ symbol before track

30Jun81-6Hol **6f** :22⁴ :46 1:11³ ft *6-5e 1175 33 32 2
DISTANCE OF RACE The race was at 6 furlongs or ¾ of a mile (the
or inexact distance (about 6 furlongs). A circled Ⓣ following the dis
on track's inner turf course; [•] indicates race run on the inner dirt s

30Jun81-6Hol 6f **:22⁴ :46** 1:11³ ft *6-5e 1175 33 32 2
FRACTIONAL TIMES The first fraction (.22⅘) is the time of the hors
front at the half-mile point.

30Jun81-6Hol 6f :22⁴ :46 **1:11³** ft *6-5e 1175 33 32 2
FINAL TIME OF FIRST HORSE TO FINISH This is the winner's final
(when the winner is disqualified, this is HIS time, not the time of th

30Jun81-6Hol 6f :22⁴ :46 1:11³ **ft** *6-5e 1175 33 32 2
TRACK CONDITION The track was fast (ft)

30Jun81-6Hol 6f :22⁴ :46 1:11³ ft ***6-5e** 1175 33 32 2
APPROXIMATE CLOSING ODDS The horse was approximately 6-
favorite; an "e" following the odds that it was part of an entry (two

30Jun81-6Hol 6f :22⁴ :46 1:11³ ft *6-5e **1175** 33 32
WEIGHT CARRIED IN THIS RACE The horse carried 117 pounds. The
apprentice allowance was claimed. When an apprentice allowance

30Jun81-6Hol 6f :22⁴ :46 1:11³ ft *6-5e 1175 **33** 32
FIRST CALL The horse was running third, three lengths behind th
indicates the horse's running position, the superior figure his total
would indicated the margin by which he had been leading the sec

30Jun81-6Hol 6f :22⁴ :46 1:11³ ft *6-5e 1175 33 **32**
SECOND CALL The horse was third at this stage of the race (at

30Jun81-6Hol 6f :22⁴ :46 1:11³ ft *6-5e 1175 33 32
STRETCH CALL The horse was second at this stage of the race,

30Jun81-6Hol 6f :22⁴ :46 1:11³ ft *6-5e 1175 33 32
FINISH The horse finished first, a nose in front of the second horse.

30Jun81-6Hol 6f :22⁴ :46 1:11³ ft *6-5e 1175 33 32
JOCKEY AND POST POSITION T. Smith rode the horse, who sta

30Jun81-6Hol 6f :22⁴ :46 1:11³ ft *6-5e 1175 33 32
CLAIMING PRICE OR TYPE OF RACE The horse was entered to
was exclusively for fillies or fillies and mares; the Ⓢ a restricted ra
the purse is given. If it is a stakes race, the name of the race is

30Jun81-6Hol 6f :22⁴ :46 1:1¡3 ft *6-5e 1175 33 32
SPEED RATING The horse's speed rating was 81.

30Jun81-6Hol 6f :22⁴ :46 1:11³ ft *6-5e 1175 33 32
FIRST THREE FINISHERS These are the first three finishers in

30Jun81-6Hol 6f :22⁴ :46 1:11³ ft *6-5e 1175 33 3
NUMBER OF STARTERS Twelve horses started in the race.

Post Position

Race Exclusively for
Fillies or Fillies & Mares

Restricted Race
(Not for Open Company)

Denotes Claim

Type of Race or
Claiming Price

Speed Rating

First Three Horses
In Order of Finish

A double-dagger ‡ shown
before the name of any
of the first three finishers
indicates the horse was
disqualified from that
position.

Number of Starters

.hT³ Ⓕ Ⓢ c12000 81 GoodHpes,LionTmr,HppyDys 12

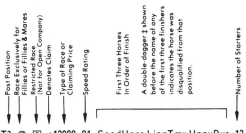

KNOW IS IN THE P.P.'s!

.hT³ Ⓕ Ⓢ c12000 81 GoodHpes,LionTmr,HppyDys 12

1.

hT³ Ⓕ Ⓢ c12000 81 GoodHpes,LionTmr,HppyDys 12

d Park (Hol.) See the Past Performance section of Daily Racing Form
s located in foreign country.

hT³ Ⓕ Ⓢ c12000 81 GoodHpes,LionTmr,HppyDys 12

gs in a mile) An ''a'' before the distance (a6f) denotes an ''about''
the race was run on the main turf course; a squared Ⓣ a race run

nT³ Ⓕ Ⓢ c12000 81 GoodHpes,LionTmr,HppyDys 12

a quarter-mile; the second fraction (.46) is the time of the horse in

nT³ Ⓕ Ⓢ c12000 81 GoodHpes,LionTmr,HppyDys 12

run in 1.11³s) In all cases, this is the time of the first horse to finish
ed first money.)

nT³ Ⓕ Ⓢ c12000 81 GoodHpes,LionTmr,HppyDys 12

nT³ Ⓕ Ⓢ c12000 81 GoodHpes,LionTmr,HppyDys 12

g. An asterisk (*) preceding the odds indicates the horse was the
coupled in the wagering), an ''f'' that horse was in the mutuel field.

nT³ Ⓕ Ⓢ c12000 81 GoodHpes,LionTmr,HppyDys 12

figure following the weight indicates that, in this instance, a 5-pound
exact amount of the claim is listed.

T³ Ⓕ Ⓢ c12000 81 GoodHpes,LionTmr,HppyDys 12

tage of the race (at the ¼ mile in this instance). The larger figure
leader. If he had been in front at this point (1²), the superior figure

T³ Ⓕ Ⓢ c12000 81 GoodHpes,LionTmr,HppyDys 12

nstance), two lengths behind the leader.

T³ Ⓕ Ⓢ c12000 81 GoodHpes,LionTmr,HppyDys 12

he leader. The stretch call is made about ⅛ mile from the finish.

T³ Ⓕ Ⓢ c12000 81 GoodHpes,LionTmr,HppyDys 12

nplaced, the superior figure indicates his margin behind the winner.

3 Ⓕ Ⓢ c12000 81 GoodHpes,LionTmr,HppyDys 12

tion number 3.

3 Ⓕ Ⓢ c12000 81 GoodHpes,LionTmr,HppyDys 12

,000 and the ''c'' indicates she was claimed; the Ⓕ that the race
en company. If it is an allowance race other than maiden or starter,

3 Ⓕ Ⓢ c12000 81 GoodHpes,LionTmr,HppyDys 12

3 Ⓕ Ⓢ c12000 81 GoodHpes,LionTmr,HppyDys 12

3 Ⓕ Ⓢ c12000 81 GoodHpes,LionTmr,HppyDys 12

FOREIGN-BRED HORSES

An asterisk (*) preceding the name of the horse indicates foreign-bred. (No notation is made for horses bred in Canada and Cuba.)

MUD MARKS

✳—Fair mud runner   ✕—Good mud runner
⊗—Superior mud runner

COLOR

B—Bay Blk—Black Br—Brown Ch—Chestnut Gr—Gray
Ro—Roan Wh—White Dk b or br—Dark bay or brown

SEX

c—colt h—horse g—gelding rig—ridgling f—filly m—mare

PEDIGREE

Each horse's pedigree lists, in the order named, color, sex, age, sire, dam and grandsire (sire of dam).

BREEDER

Abbreviation following breeder's name indicates the state, Canadian province, place of origin or foreign country in which the horse was foaled.

TODAY'S WEIGHT

With the exception of assigned-weight handicap races, weights are computed according to the conditions of the race. Weight includes the rider and his equipment; saddle, lead pads, etc., and takes into account the apprentice allowance of pounds claimed. It does not include a jockey's overweight, which is announced by track officials prior to the race. The number of pounds claimed as an apprentice allowance is shown by a superior (small) figure to the right of the weight.

TODAY'S CLAIMING PRICE

If a horse is entered to be claimed, the price for which he may be claimed appears in bold face type to the right of the trainer's name.

RECORD OF STARTS AND EARNINGS

The horse's racing record for his most recent two years of competition appears to the extreme right of the name of the breeder and is referred to as his "money lines". This lists the year, number of starts, wins, seconds, thirds, and earnings. The letter "M" in the win column of the upper line indicates the horse is a maiden. If the letter "M" is in the lower line only, it indicates the horse was a maiden at the end of the year.

TURF COURSE RECORD

The horse's turf course record shows his lifetime starts, wins, seconds, thirds and earnings on the grass and appears directly below his money lines.

LIFETIME RECORD

The horse's lifetime record shows his career races, wins, seconds, thirds and total earnings. The statistics, updated with each start, include all races—on dirt, grass and over jumps—and are located under the trainer's name.

DISTANCE

a—preceding distance (a6f) denotes "about" distance (about 6 furlongs in this instance.)

FOREIGN TRACKS

◆—before track abbreviation indicates it is located in a foreign country.

RACES OTHER THAN ON MAIN DIRT TRACK

⊡—following distance denotes inner dirt course.
Ⓣ—following distance indicates turf (grass) course race.
🅣—following distance indicates inner turf course.
[S]—following distance indicates steeplechase race.
[H]—following distance indicates hurdle race.

TRACK CONDITIONS

ft—fast fr—frozen gd—good sl—slow sy—sloppy
m—muddy hy—heavy
Turf courses, including steeplechase and hurdles:
hd—hard fm—firm gd—good yl—yielding sf—soft

SYMBOLS ACCOMPANYING CLOSING ODDS

* (preceding)—favorite   e (following)—entry
f (following)—mutuel field

APPRENTICE OR RIDER WEIGHT ALLOWANCES

Allowance indicated by superior figure following weight—117⁵.

ABBREVIATIONS USED IN POINTS OF CALL

no—nose   hd—head   nk—neck

Each horse's most recent workouts appear directly under the past performances. Hollywood Park. The distance of the work was 3 furlongs over a fast track. the date of a workout indicates that the workout was the best of the

b—breezing   d—driving   e—easily   g—worked from
tr.t following track abbreviation

The points of call in the past performances vary according to the distance of the race.

Distance	1st Call	2nd Call	3rd Call	4th Call
2 Furlongs	Start	—	Stretch	Finish
5/16 Mile	Start	—	Stretch	Finish
3 Furlongs	Start	—	Stretch	Finish
3 1/2 Furlongs	Start	—	Stretch	Finish
4 Furlongs	Start	1/4 Mile	Stretch	Finish
4 1/2 Furlongs	Start	1/4 Mile	Stretch	Finish
5 Furlongs	3/16 Mile	3/8 Mile	Stretch	Finish
5 1/2 Furlongs	1/4 Mile	3/8 Mile	Stretch	Finish
6 Furlongs	1/4 Mile	1/2 Mile	Stretch	Finish
6 1/2 Furlongs	1/4 Mile	1/2 Mile	Stretch	Finis
7 Furlongs	1/4 Mile	1/2 Mile	Stretch	Finish

NOTE: The second call in most races is made 1/4 mile from the finish; the

DEAD-HEATS, DISQUALIFICATIONS

▲—following the finish call indicates this horse was part of a dead-heat (an explanatory line appears under that past performance line).

ᵃ—following the finish call indicates this horse was disqualified. The official placing appears under the past performance line. An explanatory line also appears under the past performance of each horse whose official finish position was changed due to the disqualification.

:—before the name of any of the first three finishers indicates the horse was disqualified from that position.

POST POSITION

Horse's post position appears after jockey's name—Smith T³

FILLY OR FILLY-MARE RACES

Ⓐ—preceding the race classification indicates races exclusively for fillies or fillies and mares.

RESTRICTED RACES

◼]—preceding the race classification indicates races that are not for open company, in addition to those for state-breds.

RACE CLASSIFICATIONS

10000—Claiming race (eligible to be claimed for $10,000). Note: The letter c preceding claiming price (c10000) indicates horse was claimed.

M10000—Maiden claiming race (non-winners—eligible to be claimed).

10000H—Claiming handicap (eligible to be claimed).

ᵒ10000—Optional claiming race (entered NOT to be claimed).

10000ᵒ—Optional claiming race (eligible to be claimed).

Mdn—Maiden race (non-winners).

AlwM—Maiden allowance race (for non-winners with special weight allowances).

Aw10000—Allowance race with purse value.

HcpO—Overnight handicap race.

SplW—Special weight race.

Wfa—Weight-for-age race.

Mtch—Match race.

A10000—Starter allowance race (horses who have started for claiming price shown, or less, as stipulated in the conditions).

H10000—Starter handicap (same restriction as above).

S10000—Starter special weight (restricted as above). Note: Where no amount is specified in the conditions of the "starters" race dashes are substituted, as shown below:

A——— H——— S———

50000S—Claiming stakes (eligible to be claimed).

STAKES RACES

stakes races, with the exception of claiming stakes, the name or breviation of name is shown in the class of race column. The letter "H" er name indicates the race was a handicap stakes. The same procedure used for the rich invitational races for which there are no nomination starting fees. The letters "Inv" following the abbreviation indicate e race was by invitation only.

SPEED RATINGS

is is a comparison of the horse's final time with the track record ablished prior to the opening of the racing season at that track. The ck record is given a rating of 100. One point is deducted for each fifth a second by which a horse fails to equal the track record (one length pproximately equal to one-fifth of a second). Thus, in a race in which winner equals the track record (a Speed Rating of 100), another horse o is beaten 12 lengths (or an estimated two and two-fifths seconds) eives a Speed Rating of 88 (100 minus 12). If a horse breaks the track ord he receives an additional point for each one-fifth second by ch he lowers the record (if the track record is 1:10 and he is timed in ⁴⅘, his Speed Rating is 102). In computing beaten-off distances for ed Ratings, fractions of one-half length or more are figured as one length (one point). No Speed Ratings are given for steeplechase or dle events, for races of less than three furlongs, or for races for which horse's speed rating is less than 25.

en Daily Racing Form prints its own time, in addition to the official ck time, the Speed Rating is based on the official track time.

e: Speed Ratings for new distances are computed and assigned when quate time standards are established.

ample, Jly 20 Hol 3f ft :38b indicates the horse worked on July 20 at e was timed in 38 seconds, breezing. A "bullet" ● appearing before nce at that track.

kouts:

ily   bo—bore out   Ⓣ—turf course   Tr—trial race

e worked on training track.

ᵃ call of the running positions for the most frequently raced distances are:

Distance	1st Call	2nd Call	3rd Call	4th Call
Mile	1/2 Mile	3/4 Mile	Stretch	Finish
Mi., 70 Yds.	1/2 Mile	3/4 Mile	Stretch	Finish
/16 Miles	1/2 Mile	3/4 Mile	Stretch	Finish
/8 Miles	1/2 Mile	3/4 Mile	Stretch	Finish
/16 Miles	1/2 Mile	3/4 Mile	Stretch	Finish
/4 Miles	1/2 Mile	1 Mile	Stretch	Finish
/16 Miles	1/2 Mile	1 Mile	Stretch	Finish
/8 Miles	1/2 Mile	1 Mile	Stretch	Finish
/2 Miles	1/2 Mile	1 1/4 Miles	Stretch	Finish
/8 Miles	1/2 Mile	1 3/8 Miles	Stretch	Finish
/4 Miles	1/2 Mile	1 1/2 Miles	Stretch	Finish

from the finish.

THE PROGRAM

At ball games, the old saying is that you can't tell the players without a program. The same thing applies at racetracks. You can't tell the horses without a program.

Racetrack programs are not all uniform as to the extent of the information that they provide to the public, but most (if not all) contain certain information.

Generally, at the top of the page the bettor can find the following information on the race itself:

Distance of race
Total purse
The type of race and the conditions
The track record for that distance

For each horse, the bettor can look for this type of information:

• The number for each horse (usually the post-position number)
• Owner's name
• Description of owner's silks
• Trainer's name
• Color, age (or year of birth), and breeding of horse (sire and dam; sire of dam also is sometimes listed.)
• Certain programs indicate whether a horse was foaled in that particular state.
• Jockey's name
• Weight to be carried by the horse
• Some programs list breeder of horse (as well as state in which horse was foaled).
• Morning-line odds
• Some tracks list 1-2-3 or 1-2-3-4 selections of linemaker.
• Horses that are withdrawn from the race are listed as scratched.

How To Read The Program

A Distance of the race.

B Total purse and purse money awarded to top five finishers.

C Type and condition of race—eligibility requirements and basis for weight assignments.

D Arlington record for distance of race.

E Fastest time in 1989 for this particular distance.

F Entry. Two or more horses with the same owner or trainer count as a single betting entry.

G The identifying number of each horse (usually the post position).

H Trainer. The assistant trainer is listed in parentheses. A bullet (●) indicates the horse has a new trainer since it last raced.

I Owner.

J Description of racing silks worn by the jockey.

K Morning line odds—the early estimate of how the public will bet on a horse. The odds change as the actual betting takes place. ▲, ♦, ▼ indicates whether a horse is moving up, staying the same or moving down in class.

L Color, sex and age of the horse.

M Mojkey.

N Record of jockey in 1989 (Starts-firsts-seconds-thirds).

O Breeding of horse—shows father (sire), mother (dam) and maternal grandfather (sire of the dam).

P Weight to be carried by the horse—includes the jockey and his equipment.

Q Apprentice allowance—the weight concessions given to novice jockeys.

R The record of the horse during the current and previous year. Shows the number of starts, wins, seconds, thirds and purse money earned. M indicates maiden (non-winner) for horses making their first start. Two recent workouts are given, showing the distance, time of workout and track condition.

S Date, track, type and distance of the horse's last race. An allowance race is followed by the purse, a claiming race is followed by the claiming price and the name is shown for a stakes race.

T The horse's finishing position in its last three races, with the most recent race to the left. The figure following the slash indicates the total distance in lengths behind the winner. If the horse won the race, the figure is the margin of victory. A turf race is indicated by T.

U The horse's lifetime turf earnings.

V The horse's post position if it's different from the horse's identifying number.

W Indicates Illinois-bred horse.

X Shows medication information.

$2 TRIFECTA WAGERING THIS RACE

10TH RACE **A** 1 1/4 MILES TURF

B $200,000 Added
Distribution: Winner—$120,000;
2nd—$40,000; 3rd—$22,000;
4th—$12,000; 5th—$6,000.

C THE ARLINGTON HANDICAP (Grade I)

A Handicap for Three-Year-Olds and Upward. By subscription of $250 each, which should accompany the nomination, $2,000 to pass the entry box and an additional $2,000 to start, with $200,000 Guaranteed of which $120,000 to the winner; $40,000 to second; $22,000 to third; $12,000 to fourth and $6,000 to fifth. Weights, Monday, August 7. This event will be limited to fourteen starters. Should more than fourteen pass the entry box, the starters will be determined at that time with preference given those with the highest weights (scale considered). As many as six may be placed on also eligible list. Starters to be named through the entry box by the usual time of closing. Trophy to the owner of the winner.

ONE MILE AND ONE QUARTER (Turf)

D Track Record: PERRAULT (5), 126 lbs.—1:58⅕ (8-29-82)

E Fastest Time This Distance In 1989—1:59⅕

P.P. 1	Herbert W. Palmer			Jerry Hammond
	MAROON, gold sash, gold stripes on sleeves, maroon cap			
1	**ELLEN MARIE** ⑧	121	EUSEBIO RAZO, JR.	
	Dk b or br m 84. Hasty Flyer—Our Blue Helen by Sport Page		(412 44-61-52)	
9-5	1989 10 2 5 1 $100,000 Last Race: 25 Feb 1989 AP			
	1988 18 9 2 5 $272,120 Class,Dist: Clm50000, 7f			
♦	Turf Earnings: $2,546 Last 3 Sts: 1⁴ 3² 2¹			

P.P. 4	Herbert W. Palmer			Jerry Hammond
	RED, black blocks			
F1a	**JOY UNDERTHE FALLS** Ⓕ (L)	119	Eddie Delahoussaye	
	B g 81. Taylor's Falls—Robb's Joy by Daryl's Joy		(90 15-16-16)	
9-5	1989 10 2 5 1 $100,000 Last Race: 25 Feb 1989 AP			
	1988 18 9 2 5 $272,120 Class,Dist: Clm50000, 7f			
▲	Turf Earnings: $2,546 Last 3 Sts: 1⁴ 3² 2¹			

P.P. 2	Marc Goldish & Savoy Stable (John D. Santina)			●Robert G. Voelkner
	RED, red 'SAVOY' on white panel, red 'SAVOY' on white panel on blue sleeves, red cap			
G2	**MEGAN TYPE** Ⓕ	121	SHANE SELLERS	
	Ro l 86. Zen—Embassy Type by Buffalo Lark		(103 15-14-11)	
3-1	1989 10 2 5 1 $100,000 Last Race: 25 Feb 1989 AP			
	1988 18 9 2 5 $272,120 Class,Dist: Clm50000, 7f			
♦	Turf Earnings: $2,546 Last 3 Sts: 1⁴ 3² 2¹			

P.P. 3	Richard L. Duchossois		(M. A. Goldfine) Lou M. Goldfine
	ROYAL BLUE, gold sash, gold dots on sleeves, gold cap		
3	**EXPLOSIVE DARLING** Ⓕ	122	Abner Sorrows, Jr.
	B g 82. Explodent—Prove It Darling by Prove It		(89 11-10-16)
K 4-1	1989 10 2 5 1 $100,000 Last Race: 25 Feb 1989 AP		
	1988 18 9 2 5 $272,120 Class,Dist: Clm50000, 7f		
	Turf Earnings: $2,546 Last 3 Sts: 1⁴ 3² 2¹		

P.P. 5	Elaine F. Starzyk		Scott S. Holas
	RED, white, gold and blue crest, red 'SAVOY' on white stripe on blue sleeves, blue cap		
4L	**RED RYDER TYPE** Ⓕ **O**	**P**126 **M** KERWIN CLARK **N**	
	B l 86. Red Ryder—Cosmetic Type by Real Value		(124 13-14-21)
12-1	1989 10 2 5 1 $100,000 Last Race: 25 Feb 1989 AP		
	1988 18 9 2 5 $272,120 Class,Dist: Clm50000, 7f		
	Turf Earnings: $2,546 Last 3 Sts: 1⁴ 3² 2¹		

P.P. 6	Jeff D. Johnson, Brian Alley & Joseph E. Kasperski, Jr.		Joseph E. Kasperski, Jr.
	LIGHT BLUE, blue 'J' on yellow diamond belt, yellow diamond on sleeves		
5	**BATTLE SIGNAL** ⑧ (L)	**Q** *120	ANTONIO GOMEZ
	B g 83. Spy Signal—Battle Hand by Hand to Hand		(55 8-9-5)
8-1 **R**	1989 10 2 5 1 $100,000 Last Race: 25 Feb 1989 AP **S**		
	1988 18 9 2 5 $272,120 Class,Dist: Clm50000, 7f		
▼	Turf Earnings: $2,546 Last 3 Sts: 1⁴ 3² 2¹		

P.P. 7	Fair Systems Inc. (Vincent J. Domino) & Gollinger Stables Inc. (Thomas & James Gollinger)		Debbie Reynolds
	ORANGE, black domino, orange domino on black sleeves		
6	**NO MORE PIPE** Ⓕ	126	SCOTT E. MILLER
	Dk b or g 85. Torsion—Hand Cup by Tom Rolfe		(3 2-0-1)
16-1	1989 10 2 5 1 $100,000 Last Race: 25 Feb 1989 AP		
U	1988 18 9 2 5 $272,120 Class,Dist: Clm50000, 7f		
	Turf Earnings: $2,546 Last 3 Sts: 1⁴ 3² 2¹ **T**		

P.P. 8	Peter Canzone, et al.		Rickey B. Harris
	PINK, light blue diamond belt, light blue diamond band on sleeves, pink cap		
7	**PRINCESS KATHLEEN** ⑧ **W**	126	WILLIAM SHOEMAKER
	Ch l 86. St. Petersburg—Tinkaling by Kings Song		(16 4-2-4)
5-1	1989 10 2 5 1 $100,000 Last Race: 25 Feb 1989 AP		
	1988 18 9 2 5 $272,120 Class,Dist: Clm50000, 7f		
	Turf Earnings: $2,546 Last 3 Sts: 1⁴ 3² 2¹		

(T)Treated with Furosemide. (L)*First time using Furosemide. (0)Off of Furosemide. **X**
‌5 lbs. Apprentice Allowance
‌os. 1-1A—Herbert W. Palmer—Dennis A. Mitchell entry
‌cratched: Woy Woy, Western Playboy, Mercedes Won, Soontobeglue

HOW TO READ THE TOTE BOARD:

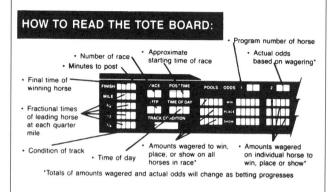

*Totals of amounts wagered and actual odds will change as betting progresses

• Generally, medication information is listed. For example, an "L" (for Lasix) or a "B" (for Butazolidin) will appear next to a horse's name, meaning that that particular horse is running with that medication.

• Some racetracks are listing such information as the horse's record—starts, firsts, seconds, thirds, and money won for the current year (and the previous year, too, in some cases), as well as the horse's finishing position in his 3 most recent starts.

The program also contains trainer and jockey standings, something all bettors should take notice of in order to learn who's performing well at that particular meeting.

2
What to Watch for During the Race

If you had two horses that you were going to bet on, I'd rather bet on the one that went out there just like a pro, ready to do his work, as opposed to some horse that is going out there wild and jumping around and getting nervous and sweated up and all that. If you have two or three horses in a race that you have to make a choice between, you could use this as a final criterion. If I were a very serious bettor, I would watch the horses in the paddock and then walking out and coming back. This is very important, because if you want to bet on that horse the next time, you have notes in your program that he came back a little sore or that he got into trouble on the first turn or the final turn. And those are very, very important notes to a serious handicapper.

> *Jack Price, trainer of 1961*
> *Kentucky Derby winner*
> *Carry Back*

". . . Carry Back is far out of it at this stage, and is moving is Carry Back. But they come into the stretch, it is still Globemaster, Four-and-Twenty and Crozier ranges up on the outside, a three-horse battle. Carry Back too far to make it —can't unless he hurries."

Announcing to a nationwide television audience, Bryan Field didn't give Carry Back much of a chance as the field swept into the stretch in the 1961 Kentucky Derby. Sharp racing man that he was, Field should have known better than to ever count out this indomitable colt.

A bit earlier in the race, while watching Carry Back going down the backstretch, Jack Price had become worried and later admitted, "At the five-eighths pole, I thought he'd died. I didn't think we had any kind of a shot."

By midway on the turn, Carry Back had begun to do enough running to give Price renewed hope. "I thought we'd finish in the money."

Down the stretch they charged, and the leaders were beginning to run out of gas. And here came Carry Back, ridden by Johnny Sellers. Carry Back charged past his fading opponents one by one. Crozier, meanwhile, made a move for the lead under jockey Braulio Baeza. "I'm passing Four-and-Twenty," Baeza once recalled, "but I see this horse coming up on the outside. Can only be one. Carry Back."

Carry Back was fourth with an eighth of a mile to go, and then he surged to third—and then second. Now only Crozier was left to be caught.

With only seconds remaining in the '61 Derby, Price didn't think his pride and joy would make it. "I was going to be satisfied with second money of $25,000 to make expenses," he said afterward. "I'm no hog."

"Crozier now on the outside in front. Crozier on the lead, and it looks for sure that Globemaster is beaten and so is Four-and-Twenty. And here comes Carry Back, the favorite. Carry Back after Crozier. Crozier with a chance to turn the tables. Carry Back charging. Carry Back coming. *Carry Back in front! Carry Back's gonna win! Here's the finish—Carry Back by three-quarters!* Crozier is second . . ."

What a great race to watch, that 1961 Kentucky Derby. What a great sport to watch, thoroughbred racing.

The best betting tip you'll ever be offered is to go to the races. Go *to* the races; don't just stop off at some off-track betting parlor or some track that is simulcasting the races from someplace else.

Go to the races to soak up the atmosphere. Get yourself some binoculars and train yourself to follow your horse all the way around the track. You can see so many things that you wouldn't see otherwise and that you certainly couldn't see by watching on a television monitor at an off-track betting facility.

It's only at the races that you can enjoy this grand sport of horse racing and appreciate it for what it really is. Watching the races in person is so much better, so much more fun, than seeing them on a television monitor. And when you're at the track, you can do so much more than watch the races. You can watch the horses come to the paddock, parade to the post, warm up, and then return afterward. You can see all of this so much better at a racetrack.

IN THE PADDOCK AND IN THE POST PARADE

When bettors take the time to walk over to the paddock, they have the opportunity to observe the behavior of the horses. An important thing to watch for is any nervous activity the horse is displaying while in the paddock. Jim McKnight, who has been riding 20 years, offers this opinion: "I'd have a tendency myself to throw a horse out that might be washed out—and mostly from nerves, not so much the humidity, because when it does get hot most all horses are going to get a little wet.

But a nervous horse most probably is running his race before he even gets to the starting gate. You'll see them, they'll be nervous and dancing around; they'll be all lathered up, more so than just a horse that's sweating because it's humid."

Like all things in racing, bettors shouldn't automatically discount the chances of a horse simply because he is acting nervous in the paddock.

For the Kentucky Derbies of 1924 through 1986, the Churchill Downs paddock was a close, cramped structure, and frequently horses became upset in the crowded conditions. In 1977, a hectic scene in the paddock caused the Derby's heavily favored Seattle Slew to become nervous. The colt kicked a hind leg and hit a board at the rear of his paddock stall. When he appeared on the track for the post parade, he was upset. He had broken out in a sweat and moved along skittishly. Yet Seattle Slew overcame the paddock scene to win his Derby.

"Some horses can come to the paddock that way and even be that way in the post parade—they'll be nervous and what have you—but they can overcome it," McKnight says. But overactivity in the paddock often is a sign that the horse will be worn out before the race even begins. And you probably won't know this about a horse unless you go to the race and visit the paddock yourself.

You should also observe the horses during the post parade to the gate. Is the horse too skittish? Is he wasting energy? This is the reason virtually every horse is now escorted by a rider aboard a "pony," actually a grown horse. In the old days, ponies rarely accompanied horses to the gate. Riders were expected to be able to take care of their horses without ponies. But times have changed, and now trainers feel that a pony helps jockeys conserve their energy for the race. These pony riders help to calm horses during the post parade. If a horse becomes rank, the jockey can count on the assistance of a pony rider instead of struggling himself with an unruly horse.

THE SIZE OF THE HEART IS WHAT COUNTS

Will the horse's size determine whether he can run a distance or is more suited to shorter races? There is a general rule you can follow, and we turn to veterinarian Manuel A. Gilman, a New York Racing Association steward representing The Jockey Club, for his comments.

"Horses that are built for distance races are long, lean, and lighter," says Dr. Gilman. "They're usually a lighter type of horse, less muscular. The heavy muscles usually tire easier. The sprinters are usually shorter and heavier and more muscular. But there are exceptions to all of it." (You should take the size and build of the horse, whether for sprints or for distance, into account when betting on any particular race length. We will discuss this point further in Chapter 6, "Horses for Courses.")

On the height of horses, Gilman comments, "If you're looking to get a horse, you should try and get one that'll grow to about 16 hands if he's a male, about 15.3, 15.2^1/$_2$ if it's a female—and that's enough." The height of horses is expressed in "hands," which is a 4-inch unit used in measuring from the withers to the ground. A horse that stands 16 hands thus is 64 inches tall. One that is 16.2^1/$_2$ hands is 66^1/$_2$ inches tall. "If they get too big," Dr. Gilman notes, "they have trouble breathing, they have trouble going a distance, and they have a lot of trouble with their legs—too much weight on them. It's tough on their legs. Going a distance, they get winded easier. There are exceptions, but the average male horse shouldn't be much more than 16 hands."

Gilman puts a mature horse's weight at 1,050

to 1,100 pounds for a male and 950 to 1,000 pounds for a female. Little horses, Gilman points out, "have to carry weight, and proportionately the weight that they put on those horses is a lot heavier for them. It shortens their stride."

But the one thing that nobody can measure by merely looking at a horse is the size of his heart. It's not how big the horse's body is. It's how much heart the horse has—and, of course, there's no way of knowing that until the race is run. As legendary trainer "Sunny Jim" Fitzsimmons used to say, "It's what one cannot see that counts." This is another reason it is so important to go to the racetrack—so you can watch a particular horse in earlier races before betting on him.

And some diminutive horses have accomplished big things on the racetrack.

In the 1929 Kentucky Derby, a gelding named Clyde Van Dusen was so small that his trainer, after whom the horse was named, made it a point to go to the jockeys' quarters before the race and tell his rider, Linus "Pony" McAtee, who had never seen the mount, not to be discouraged by the horse's size. "He can't be small enough to surprise me," McAtee assured Van Dusen. But McAtee was shocked when he came to the paddock and had his first glimpse of Clyde Van Dusen, who at 900 pounds was outweighed by some opponents by more than 200 pounds. Clyde Van Dusen was tiny, but McAtee soon learned that he was all racehorse. "He's just a pony," McAtee exclaimed after Clyde Van Dusen splattered through deep mud to win. "But he's the sweetest package of thoroughbred horseflesh I ever rode."

Northern Dancer was born May 27, 1961, making him a very late foal. As a yearling, this Canadian-bred was offered for sale for $25,000, but nobody bought him, so his breeder, Canadian E.P. Taylor, kept the little colt. Northern Dancer was proof that top racehorses can come in small packages. When he ran in the 1964 Kentucky Derby, he was 4 inches shorter than Hill Rise, the favorite. Second choice in the wagering, Northern Dancer won the Derby in track-record time of 2:00.

And then in 1968 along came a peanut of a horse named Dark Mirage to win 9 (all in a row) of 10 races and capture the 3-year-old filly championship. She weighed just 710 pounds and stood "barely over 14 hands" or "barely 15.1 hands," according to different accounts. Whichever, she was a short horse. "It is amazing that such a little thing can carry such weight and run with such elan in the stretch," William H. Rudy wrote in *The Blood-Horse* magazine following Dark Mirage's victory in the 1968 Mother Goose Stakes. "In both the Acorn and Mother Goose she picked up Manuel Ycaza and 121 pounds and won with ears pricked." These small horses made up for their size with an extra will to win. Looking for this spirit in a horse is an important step in betting to win— and a big part of what makes racing such a great sport to watch.

WATCH FOR THOSE RABBITS

Racing has a variety of strategies. Some trainers instruct their jockeys to go to the front and try to conserve the horse as much as possible. Some jockeys lay just off the pace or stay somewhere in the middle of the pack, patiently waiting to make their move at the opportune time, while others plan to surge from far back near the end of the race. The come-from-behind strategy usually needs two components to succeed: a swift pace in front to soften up the leaders and good racing luck in avoiding traffic jams. This is where something called a "rabbit" comes in. This is a horse used by a trainer to tire the front runners and so set up the race for a come-from-behind charge by a stablemate. You need to be aware of this strategy when assessing a horse before betting, and be aware of the various outcomes such a strategy can lead to.

Rabbits have been a part of racing strategy for years and years. Indeed, a rabbit—Aristides— was used in the inaugural Kentucky Derby of 1875. H. Price McGrath, who owned Aristides, planned that the colt would serve only one purpose in the Derby: to assure a rapid pace. The intention was that the early leaders would tire and would be passed by Aristides's more heralded stablemate, Chesapeake, who would rally to victory in the stretch.

As the race unfolded, Volcano and McCreery dueled immediately for the lead, followed closely by Verdigris and Aristides, while the sluggish Chesapeake lagged behind. McCreery, setting a blistering pace, led the field past the grandstand the first time. The field of 15 thundered around the clubhouse turn, and then McCreery suddenly tired out. Aristides moved swiftly to take over the lead.

Making sure that the pace would remain a torrid one, jockey Oliver Lewis pushed Aristides on as he raced down the backstretch. Approaching the far turn, Lewis then began to ease up on his mount, a clear indication that he thought his mission was accomplished. According to the game plan, it was now time for Chesapeake to come on.

As the field began to straighten out for home, McGrath was puzzled. He tried to spot Chesapeake, who was nowhere to be found among the front runners, but little Aristides was still up there in the lead, running his heart out. Lewis looked over at McGrath, standing at trackside near the head of the stretch, for some kind of signal. "Go on!" shouted McGrath.

Lewis then loosened his pull on Aristides's reins and drove the colt down the stretch. Although Volcano made a bid in midstretch, Aristides had enough left in reserve to charge under the wire two lengths ahead. Chesapeake, the Derby favorite, was eighth in a cloud of dust. The best-laid plans . . . .

So a rabbit won the first Derby. The more common outcome of this strategy, however, is for the better horse to come from behind and win the race.

In 1989, Lustra was used as a rabbit for stablemate Cryptoclearance. In the Widener Handicap, Lustra led in the early going, then was eased (meaning that, hopelessly beaten, he was ridden to the finish but not urged by his jockey), and Cryptoclearance rallied from far back to win. In the Pimlico Special, Lustra again was eased after running second in the early part, but the best the late-charging Cryptoclearance could do was finish fourth. Then, in the Suburban Handicap, Lustra was up close in the early part, then faded to 11th at the end, $33^3/4$ lengths behind the winner, while all Cryptoclearance could do was finish seventh. Finally, in the Iselin Handicap, the front-running Lustra held on until near the homestretch, then tired and finished last, as Cryptoclearance closed ground to come in fourth. The bettor should be on the lookout for rabbits and should be aware of the various possible results of employing this strategy.

WATCH THE FRACTIONS

Around the racetrack, an old adage is often repeated: "Pace makes the race." And it's so true. (We will cover pace further in Chapter 4, "Weight and Other Important Factors.")

It's a good idea to take a look at the fractions as they're flashed on the toteboard during the running of the race. The fractions sometimes can tell you what's going to happen before the race is over. If you see a front-runner setting slow fractions, then you can expect that horse to have something left for the stretch run. However, if a horse is sizzling on the front end, expect him to weaken at the end.

Speed can be dangerous in any race. A horse on the front end obviously avoids traffic problems, and sometimes if a horse opens up a big lead, he can become mighty brave out there all by himself and thus be hard to catch.

Sometimes speed can be suicidal, however. In the 1976 Preakness Stakes, a race of $1^3/16$, Bold Forbes and Honest Pleasure hooked up in a duel on the front end that was destined to burn both of them out. Bold Forbes led through an opening quarter-mile in $22^3/5$ seconds, a half-mile in :45, and 6 furlongs in 1:09. Honest Pleasure was running second. There was no way they could survive those blistering fractions—Bold Forbes faded to third and Honest Pleasure dragged himself home in fifth place as Elocutionist came on to win.

Generally, a horse can't have it both ways, running fast early and having something left for the end.

Perfect evidence of how a hot early pace can take its toll took place in the 1981 Kentucky Derby. The fastest opening quarter ($:21^4/5$) and first half-mile ($:45^1/5$) in Derby history were achieved by Top Avenger in the 1981 renewal. He wound up finishing an exhausted 19th. The pace was so swift that the race was set up for a come-from-behind victory—and that's what Pleasant Colony did, rallying from 17th place in a field of 21 under Jorge Velasquez's expert handling.

One other thing about fractions. Horses coming on at the end of a race give the illusion that they're running fast. Actually, they're frequently running slower than they were in the early pace of the race, but because the horses on the front end are tiring so badly, the ones coming from behind appear to be flying. They're not. Take Pleasant Colony. Even though he was 17th the first time past the wire in the 1981 Kentucky Derby, he covered that first quarter of a mile in about 24 seconds. He was eighth at the top of the stretch and came on to win, but his time for that last quarter of a mile was about 25 seconds. The horses in front of him were fading that much.

THOSE CLOSE FINISHES CAN BE DECEIVING

When two horses come across the wire in a close battle and you don't know which one finished first, keep in mind what I refer to as the Herb Fisher Rule. That's what I call the advantage that the eye gives to the inside horse. If the horses appear to be on even terms at the finish, pay attention to how often the outside horse is the actual winner once the placing judges have studied the photo-finish picture. Sometimes the inside horse might even appear to have won by a good head, but the camera will prove that the outside horse got there first.

Herb Fisher was the jockey on Head Play in the famous Fighting Finish Derby of 1933. He and Don Meade, who was aboard Brokers Tip, engaged in some pulling and grabbing in the final part of that race, which went right down to the wire with the two horses battling it out. Brokers Tip was ruled the winner, triumphing by no more than 2 or 3 inches, according to *The Blood-Horse* magazine.

Two or 3 inches? Churchill Downs had no photo-finish camera in 1933, and how could anybody be certain who won such a close race?

Fisher always regretted the fact that there was no photo-finish camera in those days. "I still think if they had had the photo-finish camera that they'da posted me as the winner because I was on the outside and nowadays the photo-finish camera favors the outside horse," he said in a 1974 interview. "The judges in them days always favored the inside horse. Why, I don't know, but they always did."

I started paying attention to how often observers right on the finish line think the inside horse wins in a close battle, only to learn that the photo-finish camera showed that the outside horse triumphed. Example? The Bart appeared to many to have won the 1981 Arlington Million, but it was John Henry, on the outside, who actually triumphed.

OBJECTIONS AND INQUIRIES

If interference is caused by one or more of the horses in a race, look for a stewards' inquiry and/or an objection from a rider.

The stewards watch the races to make sure that no infractions occur. Patrol judges, stationed at various points around the track, advise the stewards if they see any problems (bumping, cutting over too sharply, herding, etc.) in the races.

"It has always been understood at places I have worked that any one of the stewards can call for an inquiry, although in some cases the junior members may be reluctant to do so," explained retired steward Keene Daingerfield, the most respected racing official in America. "Since the advent of the TV tapes, it has been customary for one steward to watch the tapes while the other two observe the race. This duty is usually alternated from day to day. The inside steward may say, 'I think you had better look at this,' or 'How did it look at the quarter pole?'"

Even when a preliminary examination of the tapes would lead the stewards to believe that they aren't likely to disqualify a horse, they often post the inquiry sign when it seems obvious that the losing jockey intends to claim a foul.

3

Basics of Betting

Hardly a man is now alive who got rich playing three-to-five.

Ancient racetrack proverb

This is one of those horses who can run all day. Unfortunately, all day won't be enough time for him to finish a mile and a quarter. You've got to be discouraged when you see his jockey leave the paddock wearing a miner's helmet and carrying sandwiches.

Mike Barry's comment in *The Louisville Times* on Bold 'n Rulling's chances in the 1980 Kentucky Derby
(P.S. Bold 'n Rulling started the race on May 3, 1980, and finished it on May 3, 1980. He came in sixth at 68-1 odds, was injured in the race, and never started again. Sandwiches, anyone?)

THE ODDS

The late Frank J. De Francis, dynamic president of Laurel Race Course and Pimlico Race Course in Maryland, wagered on horses for half a century, and he may have provided the best description of what betting on races is all about.

"It's a great mental game," he once said. "In cards or dice, it's you versus the people around the table. In racing, it's 1 versus 10,000 other people at the track."

Indeed, when you're wagering on the horses, you're not betting against the track. You're betting against everybody else at the track.

The odds are established by the bettors. The more money bet on a horse, the smaller his odds. Conversely, the less money wagered on a horse, the higher his odds. The total amount of money wagered (less the racetrack's commission as stake-holder and government taxes) is paid to the bettors as winnings following each race.

The odds listed in the program's morning line are established by a linemaker. His morning line reflects, in his opinion, how he believes the public will wager on the race. For example, in the Belmont Park program for the 1989 Belmont Stakes, Sunday Silence was listed as the even-money favorite in the morning line, meaning that the bettor would receive $4 for every $2 wagered on Sunday Silence—if he won the race, that is.

The entry of Easy Goer and Awe Inspiring was listed as a close second choice in the morning line—at odds of 6-5.

Of the 10 horses in the race, Le Voyageur was the longest price in the morning line. Linemakers usually don't list a horse at odds of 50-1, but that's the price that appeared for Le Voyageur in the program's morning line.

As it turned out, Sunday Silence began the race at odds-on favorite (odds of less than even money)—90 cents on the dollar. If Sunday Silence won, the bettor would receive a payoff less than even money—$3.80, to be precise. That's derived by multiplying 90 cents by the amount of your wager ($2) and then including the wager itself.

The Easy Goer-Awe Inspiring entry, which had

been listed at 6-5 in the program's morning line, went off a bit higher—at 1.60 -1 (or 8-5 odds).

Now, there were 5 different types of bets that you could have made on the 1989 Belmont—win, place, show, exacta, and triple. In addition, the Belmont was the last of 6 races involved in the Pick Six form of wagering.

If you were smart enough to wager on the Easy Goer-Awe Inspiring entry to win, you received a $5.20 payoff for your $2 wager. The entry went off at 1.60 -1, so you multiply that times the amount of your bet ($2) to get $3.20 and then you add on the $2 wager itself to walk away with $5.20.

If you decided to play Sunday Silence or the Easy Goer-Awe Inspiring entry to place, you would have collected either way. Sunday Silence came in second.

For you to collect on a place bet, your horse must come in first or second. So your chances of collecting on a place bet are better than if you wager on a horse to win, but the payoff isn't as much because the place pool (the amount of money wagered on all the horses to place) has to be split between the winner and the second-place horse. The entry paid $2.80 to place, Sunday Silence $3.

For you to collect on a show bet, your horse must come in first, second, or third. If you wagered on the entry to show, the payoff was $2.40. On Sunday Silence, it was $2.60. And on Le Voyageur the payoff was $4.60. (That's right, the 50 -1 horse in the morning line finished third.)

The exacta requires the bettor to pick the first 2 finishers in their exact order, so if you wagered on the Easy Goer-Sunday Silence exacta, the payoff was $8.80 on a $2 bet. Picking Easy Goer and Sunday Silence didn't take a racing expert, but figuring on Le Voyageur to run third behind those two wasn't the way many people expected the race to turn out. Thus, the payoff on the Easy

Goer-Sunday Silence-Le Voyageur triple was a healthy $152.

In the Pick Six, the bettor must select the winners of 6 designated races on the card. Seven tickets were sold to those correctly picking the 6 winners on the 1989 Belmont card, and the payoff was $28,093. In addition, there was a $128 payoff for those (410 tickets) who selected 5 of the Pick Six winners.

Exotic wagering is big business these days, and racetracks all over America are getting into the swing of things by offering their patrons exactas, trifectas, quinellas, Pick Sixes, Super Trifectas, late daily doubles—you name it.

TYPES OF BETS

Win—Bettor must pick the winner.

Place—For a bettor to collect, his horse must finish first or second.

Show—The bettor receives a payoff if his horse finishes first, second, or third.

Daily double—Bettor must pick the winners of the first 2 races on the card. Sometimes the daily double is held on the last 2 races as well and is called a late daily double.

Daily triple—Bettor must pick the winners of 3 designated races. (A reminder in the Santa Anita Park program: "If no one picks all 3 winners, patrons picking 2 of the 3 will divide the Daily Triple pool, so hold your tickets even if 1 of your chosen horses loses.")

Exacta (or Perfecta)—Bettor is required to pick the first 2 finishers in their exact order of finish.

Quinella—This bet isn't quite as demanding as an exacta. You have to pick the first 2 finishers, but it doesn't matter what order they come home in.

Trifecta—Bettor must select the first 3 finishers in their exact order of finish.

Super Trifecta—Bettor must pick the first 3 finishers in their correct order in one race and the first 4 finishers in their correct order in another race.

Pick Three (or Daily Triple)—Bettor must select the winners of 3 consecutive races.

Pick Six—All the bettor must do here is pick the winners of 6 designated races on the card. As you might imagine, sometimes the Pick Six payoffs are astronomical. For some of us who have trouble picking 2 winners in a row, the Pick Six is Mission Impossible.

Pick Nine—Would you believe that this requires you to pick the winner of 9 races on the card? Good luck!

WHEELING AND BOXING

If you like a particular horse in, say, the first race on the card, you might choose to "wheel" him in the daily double with certain, or all, of the starters in the second race. If there are 10 horses in the second race, a $2 daily double wheel will cost you $20. If you wheel him with all of the horses in the second race and he comes home on top in the first, then you're a cinch to win. All you have to do is sit back and smile as the second race unfolds. Smile and hope that the longest price in the race wins.

You might choose to "box" certain horses in, say, the exacta (or perfecta). For example, if you want to box 3 horses (numbers 1, 2, and 4) in a 10-horse exacta (or perfecta) field, it would cost you $12 (6 combinations—1-2, 2-1, 1-4, 4-1, 2-4, 4-2).

BETTING ON MORE THAN ONE HORSE

No law says you have to bet on just 1 horse in a race. "There's nothing wrong with betting 2 or 3 horses in a race," says Jack Price, the man who trained 1961 Kentucky Derby winner Carry Back

BOXES AND WHEELS

By "boxing" or "wheeling," you can combine several bets on one ticket, as follows:

DAILY DOUBLE

Wheel a "key" horse in one race with several horses in the other—your ticket is cashable if the key horse and one of your choices in the other race are both winners.
Example: $2.00 Double Wheel, number 4 in the 1st race with all nine horses in the 2nd race—total cost $18.00 (9 combinations).

PERFECTA

Box two or more horses—your ticket is cashable if two of the boxed horses finish first and second.
Examples: $2.00 Perfecta Box, (3 and 5)—cost is $4.00
(2 combinations)
$3.00 Perfecta Box, 2, 4, 6—cost is $18.00
(6 combinations)
$1.00 Perfecta Box, 1, 3, 5, 8—cost is $12.00
(12 combinations)
Wheel a "key" horse horse to the rest of the field—your ticket is cashable if the key horse finishes in the selected position—either first ("on top") or second ("on the bottom").
Example: $1.00 Perfecta Wheel, 3 "on top"—with a 9-horse field, cost is $8.00 (8 combinations).

TRIFECTA

Box three or more horses—your ticket is cashable if three of the boxed horses finish first, second and third in any order.
Examples: $1.00 Trifecta Box, 2, 5, 7—cost is $6.00 (6 combinations). 4 horses = 24 combinations; 5 horses = 60 combinations; 6 horses = 120 combinations).
Key Horse Box also available—*Example:* $1.00 Trifecta Key, number 4 with numbers 5, 6 and 9—cost is $6.00 (6 combinations) and the ticket is cashable if number 4 (the "Key" horse) wins and two of numbers 5, 6 and 9 finish second and third. Key horse plus 2 horses = 2 combinations; Key horse plus 4 horses = 12 combinations. Key horse plus 5 horses = 20 combinations, etc.
Wheel two horses to the rest of the field—your ticket is cashable if the two specified horses finished in the selected position.
Example: $1.00 Trifecta Wheel, 2–6–"all"—with a 9-horse field, cost is $7.00 (7 combinations).
Variations: all–2–6, 2–all–6.
Wheel a "Key" horse to the rest of the field—your ticket is cashable if the key horse finishes in the selected position.
Examples: $1.00 Trifecta Wheel, 5–all–all—with a 9-horse field, cost is $56.00 (56 combinations).
Partial Wheels—are also available in Double, Perfecta and Trifecta betting.
Examples: $1.00 Trifecta Part Wheel, 3 with 8 with 1, 2, 4 and 9—cost is $4.00 (4 combinations) and the ticket is cashable if number 3 wins and number 8 finishes second and any of the numbers 1. 2. 4 or 9 finishes third.

Please note—
When calling Box or Wheel bets to a teller, specify the amount of the **base bet**—for example: $1.00 Trifecta Box, $2.00 Perfecta Wheel— and not the total cost of the wager.

for his wife, Katherine. "I know Kay used to bet maybe 3 or 4 horses in a race. I said, 'You're crazy. What are you doing that for?' She said, 'My objective is to beat the race, and if I have to bet 3 horses to beat the race, I'll do it.' And she was a pretty good handicapper."

HUNCHES

Unlike many of my colleagues in the press box, I'm strictly a small bettor. I've made only a couple of big scores in my life, and one of them was purely by accident.

On June 11, 1988, I liked a horse named Stop the Stage, an 18-1 shot, in the Jefferson Cup at Churchill Downs. He was the No. 4 horse, so when I went up to buy a ticket on him, I thought for a second and decided, what the heck, I'll also get a $2 exacta ticket on my age—4-5.

As it so happened, Stop the Stage won, and Cold Cathode (the No. 5 horse and the longest price in the race at 39-1 odds) came in second. The exacta payoff was $622.

I hadn't even looked at Cold Cathode's past performances before the race. After the race was over, I decided to see what this creature looked like on paper. Studying his past performances, I shook my head and said, "This horse didn't have a chance. No way in the world would I have bet on him in the exacta had I looked at his past performances before the race."

At any rate, I unashamedly went up and cashed my ticket, knowing I was the luckiest guy at the racetrack that day.

The moral to the story?

Go ahead and bet your age, or the number on the football jersey that you wore ages ago, or your lucky number, or whatever. You're more likely to collect a big payoff that way than you are if you logically try to analyze the race. It's hard to come up with two longshots in the same race when you apply logic.

ODDS AND THEIR PAYOFFS

ODDS	PAYS	ODDS	PAYS
1-9	$2.10	9-2	$11.00
1-5	$2.40	5-1	$12.00
2-5	$2.80	6-1	$14.00
1-2	$3.00	7-1	$16.00
3-5	$3.20	8-1	$18.00
4-5	$3.60	9-1	$20.00
1-1	$4.00	10-1	$22.00
6-5	$4.40	15-1	$32.00
7-5	$4.80	20-1	$42.00
3-2	$5.00	30-1	$62.00
8-5	$5.20	40-1	$82.00
9-5	$5.60	50-1	$102.00
2-1	$6.00	60-1	$122.00
5-2	$7.00	70-1	$142.00
3-1	$8.00	80-1	$162.00
7-2	$9.00	90-1	$182.00
4-1	$10.00	99-1	$200.00

THE SEVEN MOST COMMON BETTING MISTAKES

1. NOT GOING TO THE TRACK. If you have a choice between going to the racetrack or going to an off-track betting parlor or simulcasting facility, don't think twice about it. Head to the races . . . enjoy the pageantry of the sport, soak up the atmosphere, and have fun.

Going to an off-track betting parlor is like sitting in study hall in high school. Boring.

Going to the races is like recess. Exciting.

You'll become much more knowledgeable about racing and betting if you go to the track than if you merely wager at off-track betting parlors, and you will be a much more successful bettor because of it.

2. FAILING TO BE CLEAR. Pari-mutuel clerks can't read your mind, so it's up to you to be perfectly clear in making your wager. Always tell the clerk the AMOUNT of the bet, the TYPE of wager (whether it's win, place, show, etc.) and the NUMBER of the horse or horses you're wagering on. Example: "$10 to win on No. 3."

3. NEGLECTING TO CHECK TICKETS. Bettors sometimes don't check the tickets that they receive from the clerks. Don't wait until you get back to your seat to take a look at the mutuel tickets that were punched out to you by the clerk. Check the tickets immediately—and carefully—to make sure that you have the right ones. (Of course, how many times have we heard stories from people who realize after the race has been run that the clerk had punched out the wrong ticket—and yet that ticket turned out to be on a winner?)

4. DISCARDING TICKETS. A mistake that some people make is discarding their tickets before the race is declared official. If you bet a horse to win and he comes in second, wait until the race is made official before throwing your tickets away. If the horse who finished first is disqualified, then your horse is moved up to first and you collect. But you can't collect if you've tossed away your ticket and the wind has carried it to who knows where.

5. FAILING TO BUDGET. Bettors should budget their money at the races. "One of the most difficult things for a newcomer or even a veteran horse-player to do is to manage his money," says Don DeWitt, former handicapper for the *Louisville Daily Sports News*. "Don't overplay your bankroll; if you do, a horse that you might like in the latter part of the card comes up and you might end up getting some pretty decent odds on him, and here you're going to be short of funds."

How to Read a Pari-Mutuel Ticket

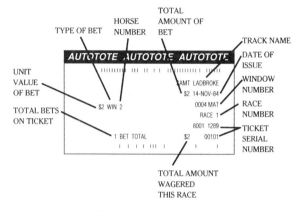

→ [arrow] . . . means "through." For example: 1 → 4 means Horse numbers 1, 2, 3, 4 inclusive.

6. NEGLECTING TO OBSERVE THE PADDOCK PROCEEDINGS. Horses are brought to the paddock to be saddled, and it's there that bettors can observe the proceedings in the final minutes leading up to the race. If a horse throws a fit in the paddock and, in effect, runs his race there by exerting too much energy, the track announcer isn't going to tell you that this horse is misbehaving so badly that he would be a terrible bet. You have to be there to see it for yourself.

7. NEGLECTING TO WATCH THE RACE. All too many bettors fail to actually watch the race. They might listen to the announcer's call or they might try to observe what's happening by looking at the race being shown on a television monitor. But the best thing to do is watch the race through binoculars. Follow your horse all the way around, notice what kind of trip he had (did he get off to a poor start or was he blocked at the quarter pole?), and then watch him return to the unsaddling area. The more you watch the horses, the more you'll learn . . . and the better handicapper you'll become.

4

Weight & Other Important Factors

Even if a horse has been running well, I don't like to bet on him if he's been carrying 115 or 116 and all of a sudden he has to pack 122 pounds. I especially don't like to take a horse that's carrying weight that he's never carried before. If you look 9 or 10 races back and you never see this much weight on a particular horse—so this is something new to that horse— I really don't like to take a horse like that.

Mike Battaglia, linemaker at Churchill Downs and Keeneland

Some years ago, a few of the tracks had an unwritten house rule ensuring that no horse could be weighted with more than 132 pounds under a mile and 130 pounds over a mile. This is contrary to the rules of racing by the definition of a handicap, which states that the weights carried by a horse are adjusted by the handicapper for the purpose of equalizing the chances of winning.

Tommy Trotter, veteran racing secretary

So many factors affect the outcome of a race. Which ones are the most important? How can you incorporate them into a handicapping strategy? Which ones are too unpredictable to bother with? Class, condition, track, distance, and pace— these are generally considered the essential elements affecting the outcome of any race. But without a doubt, one of the most important factors is weight.

WEIGHT

Weight, the old saying goes, will stop a freight train.

One train, though, that weight never did halt was the Man o' War Express. Weight never stopped him in a race, that is. But the prospect of huge weights did indeed help lead to the decision to stop racing him.

Man o' War, considered by many to be the greatest thoroughbred in the history of American racing, carried more than his share of high weights during his two-year career. Yet as talented as he was, Man o' War could be expected to do only so much in the weight department.

Sam Riddle, the owner of Man o' War, considered racing the colt as a 4-year-old in 1921, but that thought was quickly dismissed after he asked a question of Walter S. Vosburgh, the handicapper for The Jockey Club.

"Mr. Vosburgh," asked Riddle, "if Man o' War were to race as a 4-year-old, what weight would you put on his back?"

"Mr. Riddle, it would be my pleasure to handicap him under the greatest weight ever carried by a thoroughbred in this nation," replied Vosburgh.

"That's all I wanted to know," said Riddle, who shortly afterward announced the retirement of Man o' War.

In a later explanation, Riddle said, "I knew such weight would break down his legs, and I could not let this happen—so I retired him."

And so it was, Man o' War was retired with a record of 20 victories in 21 starts. Nine times he carried 130 pounds or more, including 138 in the 1¹/₁₆-mile Potomac Handicap in 1920.

THE EFFECTS OF EXTRA WEIGHT

Weights are assigned by the racing secretary in order to equalize the chances of horses of different abilities. But those assignments are always based on someone's judgment. Serious handicappers still like to look for the horse with the weight advantage.

Mike Battaglia, the linemaker at Churchill Downs and Keeneland, pays close attention to weights. "In every race, you look at weight," he says. "There are certain races where you look at it more than other races. What you really look for is a horse either picking up considerable weight or dropping considerable weight."

Theories differ as to whether weight has more of an effect in short or longer races.

"In a sprint race, if you're carrying a lot of weight, you don't really get started as quickly, you don't get up to your top speed as quickly, because of all that weight," Battaglia says. "In a longer race, you've got more time to catch your stride, and then you'll be able to carry the weight a little bit better. But in a sprint race, sometimes when you're carrying that high weight, especially if you don't get off to a real good start, you don't have that quick acceleration because of all that weight. So it can be *more* of a hindrance in a sprint than it is in a route race."

TIPS FROM RACING SECRETARIES

Here are comments from a few racing secretaries on the subject of weight:

• *Tommy Trotter* (Arlington International Race-course and Gulfstream Park; formerly with the New York Racing Association): "As a rule of thumb, most handicappers will add 3 pounds to a length up to a mile, 2 pounds additional to a mile and a furlong, then 1 pound extra for a mile and a quarter," Trotter says. "Use your judgment here as to how the horse won. Was the horse under a drive or did the score come easily? An example of this would be Kelso's winning races in the Triple Crown Handicap—the Metropolitan, where he carried 130 pounds, winning by a neck; then 133 pounds, winning the Suburban by 5 lengths: then 136 pounds in winning the Brooklyn by a length and a quarter."

• *Bruce Lombardi* (New York Racing Association): "As far as `rules of thumb' in handicapping, I usually consider 'a pound per length' at any distance I am handicapping. Recent form is more important to me than good form in a previous year or even half year. Also, the quality of the competition is seriously considered. Usually, spring and summer competition in New York is tougher than winter competition in New York."

• *Terence J. Meyocks* (Calder Race Course): "I do not follow any particular rules when weighting horses," Meyocks said, "but I try to evaluate each particular horse on its own merits. I learned this as assistant under Howard Battle, where I also learned never to weight a horse by the money earned. It is possible that a horse could win a $200,000 race but beat a bad field; therefore, this would be a poor example to consider when running against a better field. I also request that several of the officials that work for me in the racing office give me their opinions on weights for each of the handicaps that we run. It gives me different perspectives on the horses."

• *Howard Battle* (Keeneland Race Course): In assigning weights, Battle said that as a rule of thumb he uses "two pounds maybe for a length for sprinting, a pound for going long and, if they're going real, real long, then I'll cut it more, to maybe half a pound."

In addition to weight, elements which are important to consider when handicapping a race include the horse's class and condition, the condition of the racetrack, and the distance and pace of the race.

CLASS

Class is a measure of how good or bad a horse is—how well he can be expected to run. Because races are designed to allow horses of similar ability to compete, a horse will usually run in his class.

The general class divisions are maidens, claimers, and quality horses. Maiden horses are those that have not yet won a race. Claimers are horses for sale to be claimed after the race. Quality horses, also called stakes and allowance horses, are further divided into classes by the size of the purse for the races they run in.

For purposes of betting, you should consider whether a horse is running in a class lower than one he has done well in before. Usually, a horse that finishes within 3 lengths of the winner is considered at least potentially able to win in that class. This horse will have a class advantage if he competes against horses in a lower class. But he must have done well in a higher class recently. You need to be sure the horse is in as good condition when he competes against the cheaper horses as he was when he did reasonably well in the higher class.

CONDITION

Condition may be the most difficult handicapping factor to master. It is defined as the fitness, or *form*, of a thoroughbred—how prepared he is to run a particular race. The dates of the horse's most recent workouts and races and the probable effects of this activity on his current condition are highly important, because most horses only briefly retain their top form.

Generally, most experts agree that a recuperating layoff from an actual race, followed by a series of regular workouts, will result in a horse running his best race.

TRACK CONDITIONS

No 2 racetracks are identical as to soil, grading, or angles. This fact contributes to the phenomenon known as horses for courses, covered in detail in Chapter 6, "Horses for Courses." In addition, each racetrack differs from day to day, depending on weather conditions, and these variations in the track directly affect speed.

Track conditions are rated in order of descending quality: fast, frozen, good, slow, sloppy, muddy, and heavy. Tracks affected by weather conditions to be anything less than fast tracks are called off tracks. When comparing the past performances of different horses, you should compare them under similar track conditions—look at the fast-track times of the horses you are comparing, or their muddy-track times.

All horses will run better under peak track conditions. But off-track conditions affect some horses more than others, and this is where you need to take track conditions into account when betting. The horse that sets the pace has an advantage on muddy, sloppy, and heavy tracks. The horse that tends to come from behind will suffer on these off tracks because horses ahead of him will be throwing large clods of mud through-out the entire race. This affects the stamina of both the trailing horse and its jockey.

The majority of races are run on fast tracks, and most information on a horse's past perform-ance comes from his fast-track record. Some handicappers prefer not to bet on muddy tracks at all because off-track conditions make perform-ance so difficult to predict.

DISTANCE

Horse races are from a quarter of a mile to $2^1/2$ miles in length. But not all horses run at all lengths equally well.

Most of them have a very limited distance at which they run their best races. They are bred and then trained to run a very particular length. Generally, the more speed that is bred into the horse, the less stamina he will have. Some horses are sprinters: they leave the gate fast but don't have the stamina for long distances. Other horses are route horses: they have enough stamina to hang on over longer distances. Usually, a sprint is a race of 7 furlongs or less (a furlong is an eighth of a mile).

A route is any race longer than 7 furlongs. To learn whether a horse is a sprinter or a router, look at the kind of races in which he has done well in the past. Avoid betting on any horse entered in a race whose distance is not that horse's best.

PACE

"Pace makes the race." This old racing expres-sion points to another element to consider when placing your bets. Pace is the manner in which the entire race is run, as measured by the times of the horse in front. A fast pace will help some horses and hurt others. If two or three horses gain the lead and set a fast pace for the race, they will tire out battling to keep up with each other. This allows another horse to come from behind and win. Jockeys will often rein in their horses to prevent them from tiring themselves this way.

You should watch the race to see whether the jockey is holding his horse back a little; that will show you that the horse *can* run faster than he is running if he needs to. Also, watch to see whether that horse is able to respond with a burst of acceleration when the jockey finally asks him to, for the finish. You want to know how fast a horse is running, but you especially want to know how fast he is able to run.

5

How to Handicap

For a person testing his opinion at the tote windows for the first time or the recreational fan who's going to attend mainly for entertainment or hopefully, sure, for the chance to win a few dollars, I would tell him to basically bet on speed, if possible. I would say at least 75 percent of the winners nowadays are 1-2-3 at the head of the stretch. Follow the leading trainers, follow the leading riders on that particular circuit. Try to avoid betting on too many favorites. Disregard most tips that you hear.

And if you get a hunch, don't ever hesitate to wager on it, no matter what the odds are on the board, because that's one thing about horse racing: hunches sometimes work out. One thing I've always found, whenever you go up to the window to cash, they never ask you how you did it. The man just gives you your money.

Don DeWitt, former handicapper for the
Louisville Daily Sports News

There's something—and I can't explain what it is, whether it's atmospheric or whether it has to do with time lag—but there is something. I know we used to ship horses from Hollywood Park in the summertime when they had a delightful climate and we shipped in to Chicago and other places, and, boy, they just had about three or four weeks of getting themselves together again after they got back East. We'd try to send them back early enough so they'd become acclimated. I'm satisfied there is a difference.

H.A. "Jimmy" Jones,
former Calumet Farm trainer

So you want to know something about handicapping. Join the club. Some of us have been at this game for more than a quarter of a century, and we're still learning. That's the nature of thoroughbred racing. It's a never-ending education.

There have been plenty of books written about handicapping. If you read all of the different theories espoused by the various authors, you'll probably wind up getting more confused by the page. That's not to say that some of the books don't offer certain sound logic. But none of them, of course, has any foolproof systems, any mortgage-your-house-and-bet-your-life methods.

Just think about it for a moment: if any of these authors knew for certain how to win at the races, if any of them had a system that *guaranteed* results, why in the name of Jimmy the Greek would any of them write a book about it? Why would they share this knowledge with the world? Certainly, they'd keep this inside information to themselves (or possibly whisper it to a few dear, dear friends), but writing a book could in no way compensate them as much as betting on this can't-miss system would.

Of course, there are no such systems. We all know that. But there are certain rules to follow and certain people worth listening to for their advice on this challenging business of handicapping.

TIPS FROM DON DEWITT

Around the racetrack, you'll hear plenty of tips. The trick is to know whose tip to follow. An individual whose opinion is particularly meaningful is Don DeWitt, one of the most knowledgeable and astute handicappers in the business. DeWitt's selections for years appeared in the *Louisville Daily Sports News*, popularly known around town as "the finger sheet" or "the scratch sheet."

DeWitt's pick in each race was designated by the form of a finger pointing at the horse he selected. On the day of the 1986 Kentucky Derby, the finger was alongside the name of Ferdinand, with the following comment from DeWitt: "Strong as a bull in the final quarter-mile." Which is exactly what Ferdinand was in winning that Derby.

For the 1987 Derby, the finger pointed to Alysheba, with DeWitt commenting: "Bluegrass bid put him on the muscle." Indeed, Alysheba's effort in the Blue Grass Stakes—a first-place finish, although he was disqualified—set him up just right for his Derby victory.

Join us as we listen to a few of DeWitt's comments about this art of picking winners:

Is there one thing that's most important in handicapping?

"I would have to say pace is the one thing that you can pinpoint to be the most important, as far as I'm concerned," DeWitt says. "Pace basically dictates how a race is run most of the time. Fast pace most of the time helps the horses closing ground. Slow pace is going to help the horses that are up front or the one that is on the front end."

Of final times, DeWitt says: "I'm an individual who pays very little attention to final times. Of course, I'm impressed whenever a horse does something extraordinary or something better than he's ever done before, but final times don't usually impress me. To me, the competitive nature of a horse's recent opponents and recent races are more important than a final time."

DeWitt adds that post positions "are not that important per se in thoroughbred racing," but "it depends on what racetrack you're at. Racetracks vary as to whether they favor inside post positions, outside post postions, or middle post positions. Several years ago in Maryland, it seemed like there was a groove or something that developed along the inside rail. No matter what post position a horse came from, if he was a front runner, he'd try to get right over to the rail—it was so beneficial to him.

"There are just so many things that you can talk about in horse racing, but until they spring the latch and they're off, you really have no idea what's going to happen. Obviously past performances dictate what a horse should do or usually does, but it doesn't always happen that way. Form doesn't always hold true."

TIPS FROM MIKE BATTAGLIA

You can't go wrong by betting on DeWitt's tips, nor can you be led astray by wagering on the selections in the Churchill Downs and Keeneland programs. Mike Battaglia is the linemaker at those two tracks, and, like DeWitt, he's an expert handicapper, a man who knows his business.

Here's what he has to say about the art of handicapping:

"Every race is completely different, and I don't think that you're going to find one set rule that's going to cover everything," Battaglia says. "I know different handicapping theories work for a lot of people, but they all seem to me to be very, I guess, rigid. They have one set system, and that's supposed to cover everything. For me, I haven't found that to be successful. I find that you have to look at every race differently.

"If I had to pick one thing that you had to look

at in front of everything else, I guess it would have to be the class of a horse. I don't think a horse running completely out of its class is capable of winning, but I do think that horses that are in good recent form, that are sharp right now, and that maybe have been running a little bit cheaper are capable of beating horses that have been running against better horses. Look at the recent form of a cheaper horse—if he's going very well and is on the move up. Say a horse is running very well (in claiming company) for $10,000, and he's won his last couple of starts, and he moves up to $15,000 and catches a field that's just been running at that level but they haven't been running *that* well—maybe seconds, thirds, fourths, but they haven't been particularly tearing them up and winning. A lot of times I'll give the $10,000 horse the edge, even though it looks like he's out of his class, just because of his recent form. The horse has to have enough class there to start with, but his recent form is extremely important.

"When you get into the allowance horses, now that's when it gets a little bit tougher to step up. A good allowance horse that's been very sharp recently and that tries to move up into stakes company—I more or less stay away from those horses. I'll take the proven stakes horses, because to me the quality at that level is much, much, more important than, say, the class level in $10,000, $15,000, or $20,000 claiming races. You have to look at class, but with the cheaper horses, you can move them around a lot more easily—say a horse can move from the $5,000 level even up to the $20,000 level and still perform well if he's very sharp right at the moment. But when you try to make that move from allowance company into stakes company, that's when most of the allowance horses can't compete."

Battaglia also counsels bettors to go to the racetrack and observe the races carefully. "A lot of times if you watch as many races as I do, you'll see a lot of things that happen during the course of a particular race. Say, a horse breaks from the 1-post position in a 6-furlong sprint but doesn't really break that sharp, and he winds up fifth or sixth just pocketed in down along the rail with nowhere to go for half the race. In his next race, you should give that horse a little bit more consideration because he really didn't get a chance to run his best race last time.

"Naturally, if a horse gets *really* bothered and has to check up sharply, a lot of people will see that. But what I'm talking about is looking for the horses where the race that they're coming out of wasn't conducive to their type of running. Say there's a late speed horse that likes to come from way off the pace, and the last 2 times that he's been out he's caught a field with no speed at all. A horse has made the lead and stayed there all the way. And all of a sudden, you catch him in a field where there are 3 speed horses. Well, you have to *know* this from watching his past races. There's nothing in the *Form* that's going to tell you: there's nothing about the numbers—they're not going to tell you that there was no speed in the race last time out; they're not going to tell you a horse made the lead and stayed there all the way. That's something you have to observe for yourself. Say he's coming out of 2 races where he finished maybe fourth or fifth and he made a little bit of a run at the end, but there was just no pace in the race, and he comes back the third time and he catches a race where there are going to be three horses going out for the lead. They're all going to be getting tired and he's going to be able to make that late run. Well, then he becomes an attractive bet.

"It's the same thing if you catch a speed horse that's been caught up in a speed duel for his last 2 or 3 races and has been running head to head at the lead, and all of a sudden you catch him in a race where there's no other early speed. I'm going to go for a horse like that."

LASIX AND BUTAZOLIDIN

Lasix and Butazolidin are medications used on horses. Lasix, a diuretic, is used to control bleeding. (Certain horses bleed from a ruptured vein or veins in the nostrils, the pharynx, or the lungs.) "Bute" is an anti-inflammatory medication. Does Battaglia let the use of Lasix or Bute affect his handicapping? "If it's a horse's first time on Lasix or Bute," he says.

In New York, these medications aren't permissible, so it's a good idea to watch for horses shipping from that state to those locales where Lasix and Bute are allowed. Battaglia cited an example of a "horse who had been running in New York but had been stopping. You have to figure that the horse may be bleeding; if a horse is bleeding, he's not going to run well. Then he came into Kentucky, and it was his first time on Lasix. The horse just jumped out to the front and stayed there all the way. It happens frequently. You have to give that some consideration. But if a horse has been running fairly well, and it doesn't look like the horse has been bleeding or anything, sometimes the Lasix will help a little bit, but not quite as drastically as, say, a horse who has been stopping and is then put on Lasix for the first time."

SHIP-INS

One of the many factors to consider in handicapping a race is with horses that are shipped in from long distances. Some people think it's a good idea for the horse to arrive well in advance of the race, while others think it is better for the horse to get there right beforehand.

In 1980, Codex arrived in Baltimore on Tuesday night of Preakness Week, which didn't seem to give him enough time to become accustomed to the new surroundings, the atmosphere, and the Pimlico track.

D. Wayne Lukas, the trainer of Codex, was well aware of an old saying around the racetrack dealing with the shipment of horses: "I remember the old-timers used to always tell me, 'Three days or three hours.' In other words, anything in between throws you off."

If that old saying meant anything, Codex was safe because he arrived in Baltimore just over 3 days before the Preakness.

But this business of training horses is an inexact science, and there are other sayings around the racetrack about shipping. For example, old-timers in Kentucky have been known to say a horse shipping long distances should arrive longer than 3 weeks or fewer than 3 days before a race. With air transportation these days, the 3-week portion of that saying might be outdated. Indeed, many horses are flown in 10 days or 2 weeks before races, and they run well enough.

But, still, not quite 4 days? Was that enough time for Codex? Well, things turned out well enough for that colt, who had never raced outside California. He won the Preakness by 4¾ lengths.

Those who believe that it's a good idea to ship in right on top of a race can point to Last Tycoon, winner of the 1986 Breeders' Cup Mile at Santa Anita Park in California. Trainer Robert Collet was in no hurry to ship the colt to the United States from France. Waiting as long as he could, Collet finally sent Last Tycoon to this country. The colt didn't clear quarantine until the night before the Breeders' Cup. The next day he came rolling home on top at odds of 35-1.

6

Horses for Courses

Horse players are pious people with reverence for the articles of their faith, and a sacred tenet in their dogma is the belief in horses for courses. It is a fact that some thoroughbreds take to certain tracks as some men prefer particular blondes, and in Cannonade's short racing life, he has shown a distinct fondness for the tobacco-brown bridle path at Churchill Downs."

> Red Smith in his coverage of the 1974 Kentucky Derby for *The New York Times*

Turfway Park (nee Latonia Race Course) lays claim to one of the all-time "horses for courses," Perennial . . ."

> Gary L. Rogg, Turfway Park publicity assistant

CANNONADE AT CHURCHILL DOWNS

When it came to finding his way around the racetrack at Churchill Downs, Cannonade didn't need directions.

He didn't need directions to the winner's circle

either. He sure knew how to get there.

Cannonade started 3 times at the Louisville, Kentucky, track, and won each time. He captured the 1973 Kentucky Jockey Club Stakes by $2^1/2$ lengths, and a week before the 1974 Kentucky Derby, he came home 2 lengths on top in the Stepping Stone Purse. Then in the Derby, he made it 3 for 3 at the Downs, triumphing by $2^1/4$ lengths in the 100th running of America's most celebrated horse race.

"When I won the Jockey Club Stakes in the fall," trainer W. C. "Woody" Stephens recalled, "I said to Lynn Stone (the Churchill Downs president), 'Lynn, I'll be back the first Saturday in May.' And *there he was*. He ran big. He did love the track. And then I brought his brother back, Circle Home, and I won the Jockey Club Stakes with him (a $3^1/2$-length score in 1974). The family seemed to like It."

Cannonade at Churchill Downs

Date	Race	Finish
Nov. 17, 1973	Kentucky Jockey Club Stakes	1st
April 27, 1974	Stepping Stone Purse	1st
May 4, 1974	Kentucky Derby	1st

CONQUISTADOR AT BELMONT PARK

Any other horses for courses in Stephens' long career? "I would say Conquistador *loved* Belmont Park," Stephens says. "He ran a mile in 33 (1:33) in the Metropolitan. He won the Belmont. And he ran a mile and an eighth in 46 and 4 (1:46$^4/5$) in the Dwyer—3 back to back at Belmont Park. He had to love it."

Actually, Conquistador Cielo won 4 in a row at Belmont Park during that hot streak in 1982.

As a 2-year-old, in 1981, he raced at Belmont twice, winning once. The first 2 starts of his career came at Belmont, a third-place finish June 29, 1981, and an 8-length victory 11 days later. Both races were $5^1/2$-furlong maiden affairs.

The following year Conquistador Cielo rang up 4 victories at Belmont in a month and a half. For the year, he won 7 of 9 starts, and his successes at Belmont went a long way toward earning him the 1982 Horse of the Year title. On May 19, 1982, at Belmont, he captured a mile allowance by 11 lengths in $1:34^1/5$, a second off the track record. Twelve days later, he came back in the Metropolitan Handicap, 1 of only two 3-year-olds in the field of 14, and he sizzled a mile in 1:33, a track record, in winning by $7^1/4$ lengths. That race was on a Monday, and on Saturday of that week Conquistador Cielo was back in action, going to the post as the 4.10-l second choice in the $1^1/2$-mile Belmont Stakes. He won that one by 14 lengths. The following month, on July 5, 1982, Conquistador Cielo scored a 4-length victory in the Dwyer, his $1:46^4/5$ just $1^2/5$ seconds off the track record.

So the bottom line for Conquistador Cielo at Belmont Park was this: 6 starts; 5 victories by a total of $44^1/4$ lengths; an average winning margin of almost 9 lengths.

Conquistador Cielo at Belmont Park

Date	Race	Finish
June 29, 1981	Maiden race	3rd
July 10, 1981	Maiden race	1st
May 19, 1982	Allowance	1st
May 31, 1982	Metropolitan Handicap	1st
June 5, 1982	Belmont Stakes	1st
July 5, 1982	Dwyer	1st

ROUND TABLE AT ARLINGTON . . . AND KEENELAND

Round Table did it all at Arlington Park. He won sprinting, and he won going long. He won on the dirt, and he won on the turf. He set records, and he carried a ton of weight.

A great grass runner, Round Table was perfect on the turf at Arlington. He won all 4 of his starts in Arlington grass races, including 2 during his 1958 Horse of the Year campaign—the Laurance Armour Memorial Handicap and the Arlington Handicap. In 1959, he repeated in the Arlington Handicap and then won the Washington Park Handicap, a dirt race.

All told, Round Table went to the post in 12 races at Arlington, more starts than he made at any other track in his 4-year career. In those 12 starts, he rang up 6 victories, 3 seconds, and 1 third.

Though he won only 2 of 8 starts on the dirt at Arlington, he finished second 3 other times, third once, and fourth once—and he frequently was carrying heavy weight. He wasn't perfect on the dirt at Arlington, but he ran well in those races nonetheless.

Round Table set an American turf record of $1:53^2/_5$ for a mile and three-sixteenths in winning the 1959 Arlington Handicap. He established a $1^1/_8$-mile track record of $1:47^1/_5$ in winning the 1959 Washington Park Handicap. And he equaled Arlington's $1^1/_8$-mile grass course record of $1:48^2/_5$ in the 1958 Laurance Armour Memorial Handicap.

Round Table carried such heavy burdens at Arlington as 130 pounds (3 times), 131 (twice), and 132 (in his last 4 starts there).

This durable champion retired after the 1959 season with world-record earnings of $1,749,869, including $328,100 from his races at Arlington.

Round Table also distinguished himself at

Keeneland Race Course, winning all 5 of his starts at the Lexington, Kentucky, track. He achieved his first career victory in the Mt. Brilliant Purse during Keeneland's 1956 spring meeting, and he won 3 other times there as a 2-year-old. He made his final Keeneland appearance in the 1957 Blue Grass Stakes. Five days after a $1:09^4/5$ workout that was just $3/5$ of a second slower than the track record for 6 furlongs, Round Table won the Blue Grass as it had never been won before. He set a track record of $1:47^2/5$, shaving $1^3/5$ seconds off the former mark.

Round Table is the only horse ever to win the Breeders' Futurity and the Blue Grass at Keeneland. Add to that his victory in the Lafayette Stakes, plus his triumphs in the Mt. Brilliant Purse and the Steele Way Purse, and it gave him that perfect 5-for-5 record at Keeneland. Besides his track record in the Blue Grass, he came within a fifth of a second of Keeneland's track marks in the Lafayette, the Steele Way Purse, and the Breeders' Futurity. Without question, Round Table established one of the greatest records in Keeneland's history. Maybe the greatest.

Round Table on the Turf at Arlington Park

Date	Race	Finish
July 19, 1958	Laurance Armour Memorial Handicap	1st
Aug. 23, 1958	Arlington Handicap	1st
Aug. 15, 1959	Clem McCarthy Handicap	1st
Aug. 22, 1959	Arlington Handicap	1st

Round Table at Keeneland

Date	Race	Finish
April 14, 1956	Mt. Brilliant Purse (maiden race)	1st
April 25, 1956	Lafayette Stakes	1st
Oct. 11, 1956	Steele Way race	1st
Oct. 20, 1956	Breeders' Futurity	1st
April 25, 1957	Blue Grass Stakes	1st

PERENNIAL: 31 WINS AT LATONIA

Perennial seemed to be perpetually running—and winning—at Latonia, the former name for Turfway Park. He triumphed 46 times in his lengthy career, 31 of those wins coming at the Florence, Kentucky, track.

Perennial made 216 starts during his 13-year career (1970-1982) and won at Latonia in 10 of those seasons—3 wins in 1972 . . . 4 in 1973 . . . 2 in 1974 . . . 1 in 1975 . . . 5 in 1976 . . . 2 in 1977 . . . 5 in 1978 . . . 4 in 1979 . . . 4 in 1980 . . . 1 in 1981.

THE CALDER CONNECTION

Spirit of Fighter has been a regular visitor to the winner's circle at Calder Race Course in Florida, as was Hypnotized.

Spirit of Fighter has won 26 races through mid-summer of 1989, all on the Calder course and 16 of them in stakes. A foal of 1983, she's the all-time leading stakes winner at Calder. Of her first 44 starts, all but 4 has come at Calder.

Hypnotized, a 1978 foal who was retired in the summer of 1989, finished his career with 37 wins to his credit out of 110 starts. Each of his wins came at Calder, where he made all but 17 of his career starts.

Spirit of Fighter's Stakes Wins at Calder

1986—Lago Mar Handicap, Miss Dade Handicap, Burn's Return Handicap, Miss Tropical Handicap, Pembroke Lakes Handicap, Beverly Handicap, Jacaranda Handicap

1987—Miss Dade Handicap

1988—The Zippy Do Handicap, The Ruddy Belle Handicap, Princess Rooney Handicap, Miss Dade Handicap, Miss Tropical Handicap

1989—The Ruddy Belle Handicap, Burn's Return Handicap

Hypnotized's Wins at Calder

1980—2	1984—6
1981—3	1985—9
1982—5	1986—6
1983—3	1987—3

JOHN HENRY AT SANTA ANITA

Through the years, many outstanding horses have made a habit of showing up in the Santa Anita Park winner's circle, including John Henry, who captured 12 stakes on the dirt and grass at the Arcadia, California, track, and Ancient Title and Terrang, each of whom triumphed in 10 stakes there.

John Henry, the 1981 and 1984 Horse of the Year, started 20 times at Santa Anita from 1978 through 1984. The 1980 San Marcos Handicap and the two runnings of the Santa Anita Handicap were on the dirt, the other 9 stakes wins on the grass. When John Henry retired following his 1984 season, he had world-record earnings of $6,597,947. Of that amount, $1,694,550 was earned at Santa Anita, where he brought home a piece of the purse in all but one of those 20 starts.

PRIVATE TERMS AT LAUREL

In 5 career starts at Laurel, Private Terms enjoyed nothing but S-U-C-C-E-S-S. The first 4 starts of his career came at the Maryland track: a six-length score in a maiden race November 26, 1987; a one-length win in an allowance on December 15, 1987; a triumph by three-quarters of a length in another allowance, on January 30, 1988, and then a victory in the General George Stakes on February 15, 1988. As a 4-year-old, he won the Damascus Handicap on August 13, 1989, covering the mile and an eighth in 1:48^2/5, just a fifth of a second off the track record. He was favored in all 5 of his Laurel races, including going off at 1-10 in the Damascus Handicap, the final start of his career.

These examples—and there are many more—should make it clear that "horses for courses" is an important factor in handicapping a race. So much so, in fact, that most experts avoid betting on any horse without at least some history at that particular track. Most horses, they believe, do not become completely acclimated to a new course until after a race or 2. They will then run their best race. And some horses have their favorite tracks where they always seem to run their best races. When placing your bets, be aware of a horse's history at that track—whether he's run there before, whether it suits his running style, and whether he's run his best races there.

7

Great Jockeys & Great Races

One of the most heatedly argued subjects in racing deals with the amount of credit due a winning jockey, as opposed to that contributed by the trainer, or, much more importantly, the horse itself. It has been my observation that the jockey's value is generally that assigned him by today's purse distribution; i.e., 10 percent. The best rider wins occasionally on the second-best horse, rarely on the third best and never, never on the worst one. A bad rider can, of course, get the best horse beaten.

Keene Daingerfield,
former Kentucky state steward

A good rider, a top rider, will beat a mediocre rider. A top rider can ride the second- or third-best horse and win. But no one is magic on a horse; there's no such thing. There's no such rider in America who's a magician on a horse. You need the horse at all times. Being a jock's agent, I'll attest to that. The horse makes an owner, he makes a trainer, and he makes a jock. And I think that after it's all said and

*done, the horse should get all the credit, or
most of the credit."*

Victor Gilardi, long-time
New York jockey agent

TODAY'S BEST JOCKEYS

What effect can a jockey have on the outcome of
a race? In spite of the fact that some handicappers base their projections on the jockey factor,
the jockey really doesn't determine the winner.
Even the best rider can't win with a mediocre
mount. And even the best, most consistent winner loses about 8 of every 10 races in which he
competes. There is a limited amount of topnotch
horseflesh, and even the finest jockeys occasionally ride inferior animals. Additionally, every horse,
good or bad, goes through hot and cold periods.

A good jockey will make a difference on a fit
horse placed in the right race. This is why the
second- or third-best horse in a race may win—
because the best rider in the race is riding him.
Good jockeys win big races, and they usually win
close races. A good handicapper will keep this
in mind.

The above-average jockey develops a kinship
with his mount, a sensitivity to its needs and
capabilities that enables him to extract that extra
effort that may win the race.

The best jockeys are competitive, with a fine
sense of pace. They have tremendous concen-
tration and are always in top physical shape.
Finally, they are supreme strategists and are
always confident.

What follows are profiles of the best jockeys
on the circuit today—men who have proven time
and again that they can win big races with good
mounts.

Pat Day

Pat Day, born October 13, 1953, in Brush, Colorado, and brought up in the small ranching community of Eagle, Colorado, won his first race on Forblunged on July 29, 1973, in a claiming race at Prescott Downs, Arizona. The value of the race was $631, with $347 going to the winner.

Day has come a long way since then. He has led the country in victories in 1982 (399), 1983 (455), and 1984 (400), and captured the Eclipse Award as the country's outstanding rider in 1984, 1986, and 1987. His 399 wins in 1982 edged out Angel Cordero, Jr., in a battle that went down to the final hours of the year. After riding at the Fair Grounds in New Orleans on New Year's Eve, Day found himself tied with Cordero with 397 wins each. Despite horrible weather (heavy rain and strong winds), Day took a ride on a chartered single-engine craft to Delta Downs in Vinton, Louisiana, to ride that night. He brought home 2 winners to capture the national riding championship.

Day won 7 races in 1 day at Churchill Downs (June 20, 1984). He also has had one 6-win day at the Downs (November 15, 1984) and seven 5-win days at the historic Louisville, Kentucky, track. On Derby Day 1989 at the Downs, he carried a 5-win streak into the final race of the Pick Six, the Kentucky Derby, but finished second on the odds-on favorite, Easy Goer. Despite all his successes at the Downs, he is winless in 7 Kentucky Derby rides. Asked about the Derby by reporters, Day likes to reply, "I believe there's a Derby out there somewhere with my name on it. Maybe more than one."

On September 13, 1989, Day rode 8 winners in 9 mounts at Arlington International Racecourse.

Lucien Laurin, the trainer of Secretariat and Riva Ridge, said in 1989 that Day "is the greatest rider today, bar none. I think he's terrific. You watch him ride, and he doesn't seem to make any mistakes."

A patient rider, Day has come through with some stirring come-from-behind wins, including the 1985 Preakness with Tank's Prospect and the 1987 Breeders' Cup Juvenile Fillies with Epitome. Tank's Prospect, trailing by $3\frac{1}{2}$ lengths with just an eighth of a mile to go, came on to win by a head, and Epitome, more than 6 lengths behind the front-running Jeanne Jones with just a furlong left, surged home to win by a nose.

Angel Cordero, Jr.

Angel Cordero, Jr., born November 8, 1942, in Santurce, Puerto Rico, has triumphed in 3 Kentucky Derbies (Cannonade, 1974; Bold Forbes, 1976; Spend a Buck, 1985), 2 runnings of the Preakness (Codex, 1980; Gate Dancer, 1984), and 1 Belmont (Bold Forbes, 1976).

Former steward Keene Daingerfield said that of the 13 Kentucky Derbies at which he officiated, Cordero's performance on Bold Forbes stands out. "Angel seized the initiative at the break, cut out his own running, and nursed and coaxed a game horse beyond his physical parameters to actually increase his lead in the last 100 yards," Daingerfield said. "He also permitted his mount, under a left-hand whip, to drift out exactly as far as permissible, and not an inch farther. I don't think he could have heard us yelling, 'Take hold of him, Angel,' but he did it anyhow."

Just as he did after winning the 1974 Derby, following his victory aboard Bold Forbes, Cordero placed the blanket of roses on his father's grave in New York.

Laffit Pincay, Jr.

Laffit Pincay, Jr., born December 29, 1946, in Panama City, Panama, is racing's all-time leading money-winning rider, with his mounts earning more than $148 million through 1989. A powerful rider

Jockey Angel Cordero, Jr., is famous for his flying dismounts after wins. (New York Racing Association Photo)

with a good judge of pace, Pincay has won more Eclipse Awards—5—than any other jockey (1971, 1973, 1974, 1979, 1985).

Pincay, who was elected to the National Museum of Racing Hall of Fame in 1975, won 3 straight Belmonts (Conquistador Cielo, 1982; Caveat, 1983; Swale, 1984).

On November 9, 1988, Pincay became the second jockey in history to win his 7,000th race. (Bill Shoemaker was the first.) Through 1988, Pincay had 7,031 victories to his credit.

Chris McCarron

Chris McCarron, born March 27, 1955, in Dorchester, Massachusetts, came back from a shattered femur suffered October 16, 1986, to win the Kentucky Derby and the Preakness the next year aboard Alysheba. All told, he rode 1988 Horse of the Year Alysheba to 9 Grade I wins, the last coming in the 1988 Breeders' Cup Classic. "He's the best horse I've ever ridden," McCarron said.

McCarron has ridden many other outstanding horses, including John Henry, Precisionist, Sunday Silence, and Desert Wine. He's led all jockeys in races won 3 times—546 in 1974 (a record that stood until 1989), 468 in 1975, and 405 in 1980, and in seasonal earnings 3 years (1980, 1981, 1984).

McCarron won an Eclipse Award as the country's top apprentice rider in 1974 and as the leading overall jockey in 1980.

The popular rider reached a milestone in 1989 by winning his 5,000th race on July 21, and the next month he was inducted into the National Museum of Racing Hall of Fame.

Jorge Velasquez

Jorge Velasquez, born December 28, 1946, in Chepo, Panama, has won such major races as the Kentucky Derby and Preakness (both with Pleasant Colony, 1981), the Breeders' Cup Classic (Proud Truth, 1985), and the Breeders' Cup Juvenile Fillies (Twilight Ridge, 1985).

Velasquez rode Alydar in many of his races. The Calumet Farm colt won 14 races in his career, including 11 stakes. Velasquez rates the 1977 Champagne, the 1978 Blue Grass, and the 1978 Whitney as Alydar's best races, and he rates Alydar as his favorite horse.

"I love to come from behind," Velasquez said. "That's my style. That's what I like."

He led North American jockeys in total victories in 1967 with 438, and in 1969 he was tops in purse money won.

Eddie Delahoussaye

Eddie Delahoussaye, born September 21, 1951, in New Iberia, Louisiana, started riding quarter horses as a youngster. He won back-to-back Kentucky Derbies with Gato Del Sol (1982) and Sunny's Halo (1983). "He's the best waiting rider I've ever seen," said Ed Gregson, the trainer of Gato Del Sol.

Delahoussaye also piloted Princess Rooney to victory in the 1984 Breeders' Cup Distaff, Prized to victory in the 1989 Breeders' Cup Turf, and Risen Star to wins in the 1988 Preakness and Belmont.

In 1978, Delahoussaye was North America's leading rider in wins (384).

José Santos

José Santos, born April 26, 1961, in Concepción, Chile, was the United States' leading rider in money earned in 1986, 1987, 1988, and 1989, and he won the Eclipse Award as the country's top jockey in 1988.

An outstanding finisher with superb timing, he rode Manila in 5 races (all in 1986) and triumphed each time, 3 occasions in close finishes (2 noses and a neck). He calls Manila the best horse he's ever ridden. "I think it's going to be real tough to find another horse like that," he said.

His biggest thrill in racing has been winning the 1986 Breeders' Cup Turf aboard Manila. In that race, he was forced to alter course in midstretch, cutting to the outside in an impressive move, and then coolly hand riding the colt in the final strides after having his whip inadvertently struck from his hand by another jockey's whip some 40 yards from the wire. "I started riding real hard, hand riding—just riding real hard and yelling and screaming," Santos said.

In 1987, he won the Saratoga riding title, breaking Angel Cordero, Jr.'s 11-year streak.

Randy Romero

Randy Romero, born December 22, 1957, in Erath, Lousiana, was the victim of a freak accident at Oaklawn Park in 1983. He suffered first- and second-degree burns over 60 percent of his body when he went into one of the jockey quarters' heated rooms and a light bulb exploded, igniting rubbing alcohol on his body. He was told he would never ride again, but he made a comeback on July 28, some 3 1/2 months after the accident, and won with his first mount.

He was the country's second-leading jockey in 1985 with 416 wins. On the 1988 Florida Derby Day card at Gulfstream Park, he became the first jockey in history to win 4 stakes in 1 day—the featured event on Brian's Time, the Swale Stakes on Seeking the Gold, the second division of the Davona Dale Stakes on Cadillacing, and the second division of the Buckram Oak Handicap aboard Native Mommy.

Romero rode the unbeaten Personal Ensign in all but 1 of her 13 career starts. He described Personal Ensign as "that once-in-a-lifetime special thing" and "every jockey's dream."

THE GREATEST RACES OF ALL TIME

If you could put together a highlight film of the most thrilling races in the history of American racing, which ones would you include?

Well, racing is a game of opinions, and what follows here is one guy's opinion on the 11 most exciting finishes of all time. The races all depicted thoroughbred racing at its best, with close, pulsating finishes. Interestingly, Bill Shoemaker, the sport's winningest jockey, was involved in 6 of these finishes—and he won them all. Small wonder so many racing people consider Shoemaker— who retired February 3, 1990, with 8,833 career wins out of 40,350 starts—the greatest jockey of all time.

EIGHTH RACE
Belmont
JUNE 10, 1978

1½ MILES. (2.24) 110th running THE BELMONT. $150,000 added. 3-year-olds. By subscription of $100 each to accompany the nominations; $500 to pass the entry box; $1,000 to start. A supplementary nomination may be made of $2,500 on Wednesday, June 7 plus an additional $10,000 to start, with $150,000 added, of which 60% to the winner, 22% to second, 12% to third and 6% to fourth. Colts and Geldings, weights, 126 lbs. Fillies, 121 lbs. Starters to be named at the closing times of entries, Thursday, June 8. The winning owner will be presented with the August Belmont Memorial Cup and trophies will be presented to the winning trainer and jockey. (Closed Wednesday, February 15, 1978 with 268 nominations.)

Value of race is $184,300, value to winner $110,580, second $40,546, third $22,116, fourth $11,058. Mutuel pool $1,186,662. OTB pool $1,389,646.

Last Raced	Horse	Eqt.A.Wt	PP	¼	½	1	1¼	Str	Fin	Jockey	Odds $1
20May78 ⁸Pim¹	Affirmed	3 126	3	1¹	1¹	1½	1ʰᵈ	1ʰᵈ	1ʰᵈ	Cauthen S	.60
20May78 ⁸Pim²	Alydar	3 126	2	3¹½	2¹	2⁵	2¹²	2¹³	2¹³	Velasquez J	1.10
28May78 ⁸Bel²	Darby Creek Road	3 126	1	5	5	3½	3⁴	3⁷³/₄	3⁷³/₄	Cordero A Jr	9.90
22May78 ⁵Aqu⁹	Judge Advocate	3 126	4	2¹¹/₂	3²¹/₂	4³	5	4⁴	4¹¹/₄	Fell J	30.10
29May78 ⁸Mth²	Noon Time Spender b	3 126	5	4¹	4³	3½	4ʰᵈ	5	5	Hernandez R	38.40

OFF AT 5:43, EDT. Start good, Won driving. Time, :25, :50, 1:14, 1:37²/₅, 2:01³/₅, 2:26⁴/₅. Track fast.

$2 Mutuel Prices:

3–(C)–AFFIRMED		3.20	2.10	
2–(B)–ALYDAR			2.20	
1–(A)–DARBY CREEK ROAD				

Ch. c, by Exclusive Native—Won't Tell You, by Crafty Admiral. Trainer Barrera Lazaro S. Bred by Harbor View Farm (Fla).

AFFIRMED went right to the front and was rated along on the lead while remaining well out from the rail. He responded readily when challenged by ALYDAR soon after entering the backstretch, held a narrow advantage into the stretch while continuing to save ground and was under left-handed urging to prevail in a determined effort. ALYDAR, away in good order, saved ground to the first turn. He came out to go after AFFIRMED with seven furlongs remaining, raced with that rival to the stretch, reached almost even terms with AFFIRMED near the three-sixteenths pole but wasn't good enough in a stiff drive. DARBY CREEK ROAD, unhurried while being outrun early, moved around horses while rallying on the far turn but lacked a further response. JUDGE ADVOCATE broke through before the start and was finished at the far turn. NOON TIME SPENDER raced within striking distance for a mile and gave way.

Owners—1, Harbor View Farm; 2, Calumet Farm; 3, Phillips J W; 4, Phipps O; 5, Miami Lakes Ranch.

Trainers—1, Barrera Lazaro S; 2, Veitch John M; 3, Reading J I; ...

Join us as we take a look at these 11 races and just imagine what they would look like spliced together on 1 reel.

The 1978 Belmont Stakes

The best race I've ever seen was the 1978 Belmont Stakes, featuring Affirmed and Alydar. Those two had met in 8 previous races, with Affirmed beating Alydar in 6 of them, including the Kentucky Derby and the Preakness. All told, in those 8 races, Affirmed held an advantage of only about 3 lengths over Alydar.

As post time for the race neared, everybody seemed to sense that something big was about to happen. The dramatic confrontation between Affirmed and Alydar was much like a heavyweight championship match. The arch-rivals were preparing to do battle, and the tension was high.

At 5:43 P.M., starter George Cassidy sent the field on its way. Affirmed took the early lead with Judge Advocate running second and Alydar third. Steve Cauthen, the 18-year- old rider on Affirmed, moved his colt through the first quarter in 25 seconds, exceedingly slow time. Affirmed took another 25 seconds to cover the next quarter. The pace was slow, and the longer Cauthen was able to keep Affirmed taking it easy on the lead, the better it was for him. But Jorge Velasquez, the rider on Alydar, had had enough of these slow-down tactics and he did what he had to do—he went after Affirmed. Racing down the backstretch, Alydar drew up alongside Affirmed. No introductions were needed. These two colts had met before . . .and now the race was on. They covered the third quarter in 24 seconds; the fourth in :23^2/5.

Affirmed and Alydar rounded the sweeping far turn, drawing away from their hopelessly beaten opponents, and reached the top of the stretch locked together in a 2-horse duel that was so reminiscent of their past races.

Cauthen went to the whip. He hit Affirmed

some 9 times right-handed from the top of the stretch to about the three-sixteenths pole.

In a smart riding tactic, Velasquez moved Alydar so close to Affirmed that Cauthen could no longer use the whip on the right side. Cauthen had never whipped Affirmed on the left side, but now he had no choice. Alydar had taken a slight lead on Affirmed near the three-sixteenths pole, and Cauthen had to do something to get his colt moving. So he switched his whip to his left hand, and he went to work.

The fans were yelling and screaming as the 2 horses thundered toward the finish line, running side by side, each reaching out and straining, each determined to beat the other. It was a rousing finish, a stirring windup to a brilliant Triple Crown series. Clearly, any one with a heart condition had no business watching a race as breathtaking as this one.

Affirmed was tired, but he had come too far now to call it quits. He dug in even more and fought. Alydar was in a fighting mood, too, and here they came, Affirmed on the inside and Alydar on the outside, just yards away from the finish, drawing closer and closer to the wire.

Finally, the race was over . . . and the finish was close. Close enough for the "photo finish" sign to be lit up. But not so close that those with the right vantage point didn't know who had won.

Charlie Rose, the Calumet Farm exercise rider, knew. He had been in the sport for 31 years, and for the first time, tears came to his eyes after a race.

Velasquez knew, too.

So did Cauthen, who thrust his left hand up high in a victory salute immediately after the finish. It was only appropriate that he raised his left hand in victory because it was Affirmed's response to left-handed whipping that had gained the nod.

It was that emotional—for both the winning

The 1988 Breeders' Cup Distaff.
Personal Ensign, Goodbye Halo,
Winning Colors. Breeders' Cup Photo
by Janeart, Ltd.

and losing camps.

The numbers went up on the board: 3-2-1-4.

It was 5:48, and now everybody knew. Affirmed had won the Triple Crown.

The 1988 Breeders' Cup Distaff

It came down to the last stride of her career. The very last stride.

Personal Ensign, unbeaten in her first 12 career starts, was making her final appearance on Breeders' Cup Day at Churchill Downs in 1988. She was the 1-2 favorite to win the $1^1/_8$-mile Breeders' Cup Distaff, but with just an eighth of a mile to go, her chances didn't look good. She was third, a full 4 lengths behind the leader, Winning Colors, who had won the Kentucky Derby earlier in the year.

On she came, Personal Ensign determinedly bidding to get to the front. It came down to the last stride of her career, and she did it, getting up in the final jump to edge Winning Colors by a nose.

D. Wayne Lukas, trainer of Winning Colors, recalls that race like this: "It almost gave us the best of both worlds. A lot of people hated to see Winning Colors beat after she ran so well. On the other hand, the fact that the other filly won was very popular because, even for myself, it was wonderful to have a filly run that well all her career and then finish it out that way. We feel that, had we had a good fast track, we probably would have won. I don't think they would ever have caught us. But that was certainly one of the best of all time—that was a super race."

The 1962 Travers

Jaipur and Ridan went the entire mile and a quarter battling it out in the torrid 1962 Travers at Saratoga. Ridan, ridden by Manuel Ycaza, led by a half-length after a quarter-mile, and by a head after a half-mile and after three-quarters. Jaipur, with Shoemaker up, was in front by a head after a mile and after a mile and an eighth. When the two colts raced under the wire, it was Jaipur by a nose. Ridan had fought to the very end.

"I knew Jaipur beat us," said LeRoy Jolley, the trainer of Ridan. "I saw The Shoe drop his head down right at the finish."

The time of 2:01^3/5 equaled a 16-year-old track record and broke the Travers record of 2:01^4/5 set 42 years earlier by none other than Man o' War.

"Generally speaking," Dave Alexander wrote in *The Blood-Horse*, "I've never known so many horsemen to disagree so widely about a finish. They were still discussing it and arguing about it at the Lantern Lodge near the track at Sunday breakfast. They were discussing it in Saratoga bars and under Saratoga's elms. Folks who love racing will be discussing it a hundred years from now, I suspect, because it must go down in the history books as one of the most thrilling contests the turf has produced."

The 1978 Preakness

A record Preakness crowd of 81,261 turned out on a hot day in 1978 at Pimlico and was treated to a hot battle between those old rivals, Affirmed and Alydar.

At the start, Track Reward and Affirmed went for the early lead. Alydar, as expected, was much closer to the pace than he had been in the Kentucky Derby. Affirmed proceeded to move past Track Reward, setting some slow fractions. Alydar was perfectly placed and closed in on Affirmed rounding the far turn.

At the top of the stretch, Alydar was rolling, moving up to challenge Affirmed. Velasquez believed that he would win the race. Yet he knew that Affirmed liked to wait for horses when he was in front. Velasquez was fully aware that he still had·a battle on his hands coming down the Pimlico stretch.

It had now developed into strictly a 2-horse race, Affirmed leading and Alydar coming on. The crowd was going wild.

They were nearing the finish now, a classic duel between 2 horses going as fast as their legs and bloodlines would carry them, 2 horses running their hearts out, 2 horses staging a memorable battle.

Affirmed still was leading, but Alydar had dead aim on him. All Alydar had to do was pass his rival and go on to win the race.

But he couldn't.

At the finish, it was the same old story: Affirmed first, Alydar second. The margin of victory was a neck. A long neck. And it was a long way back—$7^1/2$ lengths—to Believe It in third.

The race was a great one, and up in the press box many writers were all shook up. Mike Barry of *The Louisville Times* was nearly incoherent. A veteran turf writer on one side of him said, "I'm wound up so tight I can't breathe!" A man on the other side of Barry said, "I was afraid my heart was gonna stop."

Indeed, the '78 Preakness produced such a stirring finish that Barry called it the most exciting race he'd ever seen. "My God, I was dying every inch," he said.

The 1981 Arlington Million

"It was probably the greatest race I've ever ridden in. Not only because I won it. It was a great finish between 2 great horses in a great field."

That appraisal came from none other than 50-year-old Bill Shoemaker, the winningest jockey in history, and it came following his triumph on John Henry in the 1981 Arlington Million, the inaugural running of this showcase international race.

"I knew I had enough horse," Shoemaker said. "I just hoped I had enough ground."

Ground was running out on John Henry, the veteran 6-year-old gelding, in this $1^1/4$-mile race run on a soft-turf course at Arlington Park. With a furlong left, The Bart, ridden by Eddie Delahoussaye, held a length lead over Key to Content, John Henry, and Madam Gay, all tightly bunched. "I thought I could beat The Bart handily at that point," Shoemaker said. "Quickly, though, I saw that Eddie had more horse left than I first thought he had. At the wire, I felt that I had got up to nip him, but pulling up, I said, 'I dunno, that was awfully close.'"

Said Delahoussaye: "My horse just ran a super race. It was better than he had ever run before. At the sixteenth pole, I thought we were going to make it. I think I came as close to winning as I could."

Angel Cordero, Jr., who finished sixth on Argument, said: "We saw today why Shoe is the greatest rider in the world. I never thought he could catch that horse in front."

The 1976 Marlboro Cup

"It was one of the greatest races I've ever been in or seen."

If this comment sounds like a replay of what Shoemaker said following the 1981 Million, well, that's what happens when you ride 6-year-old geldings to dramatic come-from-behind victories. This time Shoemaker made this comment following his victory aboard Forego in the 1976 Marlboro Cup at Belmont Park.

In a breathtaking finish, Forego overtook Honest Pleasure at the wire to win by a head. Forego, the old warrior, carried a staggering 137 pounds, compared with 119 on Honest Pleasure, a 3-year-old colt.

"I didn't have any real trouble," Shoemaker said, "but at the three-eighths pole, I didn't think I would be in the money. He wasn't taking hold of the bit. But in the stretch, he gave me that run, and it's a beaut."

It took a beaut of a stretch run to overhaul

Honest Pleasure, who held a 2$\frac{1}{2}$-length lead over second-place Dance Spell with a quarter of a mile to go. Forego was sixth at that point . . . and down the stretch he charged.

"He was laboring, sure, but he was running and giving his all," Shoemaker said. "I knew at the furlong pole (an eighth of a mile from the wire) I had a shot at it, and, boy, I did. That's a real racehorse."

A real racehorse, indeed.

With the crowd of 31,716 roaring, the favored Forego came charging up on the outside to win the 1$\frac{1}{4}$-mile race on a sloppy racing strip in 2 minutes flat.

The 1978 Jockey Club Gold Cup

Exceller won this race over two Triple Crown champions—Seattle Slew and Affirmed. Joe Hirsch, the Eclipse Award-winning columnist for The *Daily Racing Form*, summed up this race best by writing that in years to come when the story of this Jockey Club Gold Cup is told, "this memorable encounter will be compared with the great races of our time, such as the 1957 Trenton Handicap at Garden State Park, when Bold Ruler beat Gal-lant Man and Round Table; the 1959 Woodward Stakes . . . when Sword Dancer beat Hillsdale and Round Table; and the 1967 Woodward, when Damascus beat Buckpasser and Dr. Fager."

Hirsch wrote that, in defeat, "Seattle Slew ran perhaps his greatest race, and there isn't much doubt that at this time he is the best horse in the country and possibly the world."

Indeed, Seattle Slew did distinguish himself in defeat. After 6 furlongs in 1:09$\frac{2}{5}$, a clocking that track announcer Chic Anderson described to a national television audience as "unbelievable" in a 1$\frac{1}{2}$-mile race, Seattle Slew would have had every right to call it quits against Exceller, who had come with a rush from far off the pace under

Shoemaker's handling. Exceller took the lead in the stretch, but Seattle Slew dug in and battled back in a remarkable effort. At the wire, though, it was Exceller by a nose.

But as Eclipse Award-winning columnist Billy Reed wrote: "Slew, even in losing, came up with a true-grit performance that proved his class and courage beyond doubt."

The 1987 Breeder's Cup Classic

Through the years, Kentucky Derby winners have run against each other in 42 races, and the most exciting finish in any of these battles was the 1987 Breeders' Cup Classic at Hollywood Park. Ferdinand, the 1986 Derby victor, triumphed by a nose over Alysheba, the 1987 Derby winner. With Shoemaker timing his move perfectly, the favored Ferdinand moved past Judge Angelucci, and then held off a late charge by Alysheba to win the $1\frac{1}{4}$-mile race. This race marked the only time in history that two Derby winners have finished 1-2 in the same race with only a whisker separating them.

Ferdinand was a colt who would relax once he got in front, and the footnotes in the *Daily Racing Form's* chart pointed out that Shoemaker waited "as long as possible to ask his mount to go for the lead."

Said Shoemaker: "I didn't want to make the lead too soon, but I was kind of worried at about the sixteenth pole whether I was going to get by the Judge or not. I saw Alysheba coming up on the outside, and I just waited, waited, waited, then I shook my stick at him and let him go to the lead. He saw Alysheba coming in just enough time to put in a little extra effort, and he got the job done."

The 1959 Kentucky Derby

A crowd of 72,951 turned out in 94-degree weather for the 1959 Kentucky Derby, and what they were

The 1987 Breeders' Cup Classic.
Alysheba, Ferdinand at the finish.
Breeders' Cup Photo by Bill Straus.

treated to was one of the hottest battles on record. The noise was deafening as the field swung into the stretch, particularly when thousands of women started screaming and shouting after the track announcer called out that Silver Spoon, a filly, was racing in third place.

If Silver Spoon looked good at that point, looking even better were Tomy Lee and Sword Dancer, the 2 front-running horses. At the same time that the women were shrieking, another yell went up, but the only person who could hear it was Bill Boland, who was moving Sword Dancer past Tomy Lee, ridden by Shoemaker, and into the lead near the quarter pole. Shoemaker, thinking that Tomy Lee was finished and wouldn't be able to regain the lead, called out to Boland, "Good luck, go on and get it."

To Shoemaker's surprise, just when he thought Sword Dancer was about to pull away, Tomy Lee dug in and came back. With the crowd yelling itself hoarse, Sword Dancer and Tomy Lee hooked up in a dramatic stretch duel. Passing the three-sixteenths pole, Tomy Lee came out into Sword Dancer, who was leading by half a length, and then near the eighth pole, Sword Dancer slammed in against Tomy Lee, which caused him to change leads and gave him the needed impetus in the final furlong.

With 50 yards to go, Sword Dancer, still holding the lead, looked like he was going to hang on. But Shoemaker, in a brilliant display of riding, called on the indomitable Tomy Lee for just 1 final surge, and the English-bred colt charged back to win by a nose.

Boland promptly claimed a foul against Tomy Lee. The stewards studied the patrol film but disallowed the claim . . . and it was official—Tomy Lee was the winner of the most exciting stretch battle in Kentucky Derby history.

The 1930 Kentucky Jockey Club Stakes

The 1930 Kentucky Jockey Club Stakes had all the ingredients of a memorable horse race.

It had 2 starters, Twenty Grand and Equipoise, who would earn their places in the National Museum of Racing Hall of Fame.

It had 2 jockeys also destined for the Hall of Fame—Charley Kurtsinger, who was known as the "Flying Dutchman," and Raymond "Sonny" Workman.

And it had a torrid stretch duel that resulted in a narrow victory for Twenty Grand in sensational time. Not only was it a track record, but at that time it was the fastest mile ever run by 2-year-olds in America—a minute and 36 seconds.

With 2 scratches, a field of 7 went to the post. Equipoise was sent off as the favorite at 76 cents on the dollar (payoffs were to the penny in those days), and Twenty Grand was second choice at $2.77-1.

Don Leon took the early lead, with Equipoise second and Twenty Grand dropping back to last. Twenty Grand then began moving and was second after 6 furlongs, trailing Equipoise. With the field now straightened out for the stretch run, the race was strictly a 2-horse affair, Equipoise leading and Twenty Grand coming on.

Twenty Grand edged into a head lead at the stretch call, but he was unable to pull away. As a great horse will do, Equipoise dug in after losing the lead in the homestretch and, with Workman cracking him with his whip, the determined colt put up quite a battle in the final yards. At the wire, however, it was Twenty Grand winning by a margin reported as either a nose or a neck.

So superior were Twenty Grand and Equipoise that it was a full 10 lengths back to Knight's Call in third place.

1989 Preakness

Alydar lost the 1978 Preakness in a thrilling finish,

and 11 years later, his son, Easy Goer, would go down to defeat in a torrid battle with Sunday Silence in this second leg of the Triple Crown. With a record Preakness crowd of 90,145 looking on, Sunday Silence won by a nose.

Sunday Silence, ridden by Patrick Valenzuela, held a narrow margin over Easy Goer, with Pat Day up, turning for home. "I thought I was going to put him away right there," Valenzuela said, "but Pat had horse left. He went right with me, and it was a hell of a race right to the wire."

Sunday Silence led by a head at the stretch call, then Easy Goer moved in front briefly nearing the last sixteenth . . . and then it was Sunday Silence who prevailed in a brilliant finish.

Jack, Price, the man who trained 1961 Kentucky Derby and Preakness winner Carry Back, has been watching races for more than 60 years, and he calls the '89 Preakness the best he's ever seen. "It was a tremendous race and a pleasure to watch."

Joe Hirsch, esteemed executive columnist for the *Daily Racing Form*, declared that this Preakness "was climaxed by perhaps the most exciting finish in the 114-year history of the race."

8

The Great Trainers

*My father was probably as great a horseman
as ever lived. I mean, just a pure horseman. He
was a genius, that's all you can say, with a
horse, with the condition of a horse—their legs
and everything. He never had the money to
buy good horses. He bought other people's
horses that they wrecked and brought them
back to the races.*

> Jack Van Berg, Hall of Fame trainer

*I consider Charlie Whittingham one of the great
trainers in my time, and I go back quite a ways
with the likes of Ben Jones, Max Hirsch, Sunny
Jim Fitzsimmons, and many other greats. I put
Charlie right there with all of them.*

> Eddie Arcaro, Hall of Fame jockey

Often, trainers have as much to do with the outcome of big races as the horses they are training.
Bettors who wish to understand horses and make
money at the track should recognize the great
importance of trainers.

Training fulfills the promise made by breeding. A horse's outstanding parentage and promise mean nothing in the hands of an untalented trainer. A great horse must have a good trainer in order to realize his potential. And even a problem horse can improve greatly under a talented trainer.

The best trainers know how to prepare a horse for a specific race. And they never enter a horse in a race where he doesn't belong—out of his class, or in a race of the wrong distance.

The best horseman usually wins with about 20 per cent of the horses he sends on to the track. Keep in mind that trainers, like any competitors, have hot streaks and cold spells. Astute handicappers learn to recognize and analyze these streaks.

Knowing which horsemen are competent and which are not makes a good handicapper. Over time, the most successful bettors come to understand the different trainers' strengths and weaknesses and then can apply that knowledge to a handicapping strategy.

In order to give you an idea of what to look for as you study different trainers, here are profiles of some of the greatest horsemen in thoroughbred racing.

Woody Stephens

Woodford Cefis Stephens, born on September 1, 1913, in Stanton, Kentucky, remembers his roots.

Just ask the legendary trainer what Kentucky means to him, and he'll reply, "We'll put it this way: I was born there, and I came up there as just a real little, poor country boy. And, as I began to get a little bit older and my dad let me have a pony of my own and ride him, I learned to love him—and love those horses. Then I began to hear about the racetrack, about jockeys. I never thought about trainers. I learned to gallop horses. And then I was able to ride my first winner at Hialeah on opening day of 1931.

"Somebody asked me, 'What was your biggest

thrill—ever?' I said, 'The 100th Kentucky Derby in front of the home folks, down-home, to win that 100th running.' And I said, 'The 5 Belmonts are beautiful, but I can never forget the one back home, the 100th Derby.'"

Woody Stephens has made quite a name for himself since his early days in Kentucky. He went to New York with his wife, Lucille, some 45 years ago. "When we crossed that Hudson into New York, we had $400, and I told Lucille I didn't know what might happen."

What happened was that Stephens established a record that has made him one of the most successful, one of the most respected, one of the most popular trainers in the history of the sport. And even though Stephens has lived in New York all these years, he has never forgotten his way back to Kentucky.

He's returned to Kentucky to win 2 renewals of the Kentucky Derby—with Cannonade for that memorable 100th running in 1974 and with Swale in 1984—and to finish 2nd in the Churchill Downs classic 3 times—with Never Bend in 1963, Stephan's Odyssey in 1985, and Forty Niner in 1988. He's also won the Kentucky Oaks a record 5 times—3 for the Cain Hoy Stable of Captain Harry F. Guggenheim—with Hidden Talent (a division in 1959), Make Sail (1960), and Sally Ship (1963). Woody's other triumphs in the Oaks have come with White Star Line (1978) and Heavenly Cause (1981). Altogether, he's won 17 stakes races at Churchill Downs through 1989.

Stephens is no stranger to the winner's circle at Keeneland Race Course either. He's captured a record 19 stakes at the Lexington, Kentucky, track through 1989.

Stephens's unprecedented streak of 5 straight Belmont Stakes victories is truly remarkable, a feat that ranks among the greatest in the history of all sports. He won his first Belmont in 1982 with Conquistador Cielo, who went on to earn the Horse of the Year title that season, and then the veteran trainer sent out the following winners in "The Test of the Champion"—Caveat (1983), Swale (1984), Crème Fraîche (1985), and Danzig Connection (1986).

Woody also has won the Preakness once—in 1952 with Blue Man—and he trained Bald Eagle to back-to-back victories in the Washington, D. C., International (1959-1960). In additon, he's trained 11 champions.

Stephens has done virtually all there is to do in racing, and he's been honored accordingly:

In 1976, he was inducted into the National Museum of Racing Hall of Fame at Saratoga Springs, New York.

In 1983, he won the Eclipse Award as the country's leading trainer.

In 1985, he was the honored guest at the Thoroughbred Club of America's annual testimonial dinner in Lexington, Kentucky.

And in 1989, he was honored with a "Woody Stephens Day" in Midway, the ol' Kentucky town where he grew up.

Woody Stephens's 5 Straight Wins in the Belmont Stakes

Year	Winner	Jockey	Time
1982	Conquistador Cielo	Laffit Pincay, Jr.	2:28^1/$_5$ (sloppy)
1983	Caveat	Laffit Pincay, Jr.	2:27^4/$_5$ (fast)
1984	Swale	Laffit Pincay, Jr.	2:27^1/$_5$ (fast)
1985	Crème Fraîche*	Eddie Maple	2:27 (muddy)
1986	Danzig Connection	Chris McCarron	2:29^4/$_5$ (sloppy)

* Crème Fraîche was coupled with Stephan's Odyssey, who finished 2nd.

Winning margins—Conquistador Cielo (14 lengths), Caveat (3½ lengths), Swale (4 lengths), Crème Fraîche (half-length), Danzig Connection (1¼ lengths).

Charlie Whittingham

Charlie Whittingham, born April 13, 1913, in San Diego, is the king of California trainers. He has won the prestigious Santa Anita Handicap 8 times (no other trainer has won it more than twice), and he has triumphed in 14 runnings of the San Juan Capistrano, including the 1989 running with Nasr El Arab.

Whittingham has trained more than 230 stakes winners and is the all-time leader in stakes victories with more than 575. He recorded his 500th stakes victory with Ferdinand in the 1987 Cabrillo Handicap at Del Mar. In the 1973 Hollywood Gold Cup, he saddled 3 horses for 3 owners, and they finished 1st (Kennedy Road), 2nd (Quack), and 3rd (Cougar II).

He grew up in San Diego near the old Tijuana racetrack in Mexico, and worked as a groom, jockey's agent, and assistant trainer. After working for trainer Horatio Luro in the mid-1930s, he served in the Marine Corps during World War II. He was a member of the Second Division, which saw action at Guadalcanal.

Nicknamed "The Bald Eagle" and "Sir Charles," Whittingham was elected to the National Museum of Racing Hall of Fame in 1974 and won the Eclipse Award as the country's top trainer in 1971, 1982, and 1989. He has led the country in purse winnings 7 years (1970–1973, 1975, 1981, and 1982). He is the oldest trainer to win the Kentucky Derby, having done it twice—at the age of 73 with Ferdinand in 1986 and at 76 with Sunday Silence in 1989.

Hall of Fame trainers Charlie Whittingham (left) and W.C. "Woody" Stephens

A trainer known for his patience with horses, Whittingham has trained 9 champions, including 3 Horses of the Year (Ack Ack, 1971, Ferdinand, 1987, and Sunday Silence, 1989).

Says fellow trainer Jack Van Berg: "Charlie is one of the finest friends, competitors, horse trainers, and gentlemen that anyone could expect to meet. In plain words, they don't make them any better than Charlie."

Charlie Whittingham's Wins in the Santa Anita Handicap

Year	Horse	Jockey	Weight
1957	Corn Husker	Ralph Neves	105
1967	Pretense	Bill Shoemaker	118
1971	Ack Ack	Bill Shoemaker	130
1973	Cougar II	Laffit Pincay, Jr.	126
1975	Stardust Mel	Bill Shoemaker	123
1985	Lord at War	Bill Shoemaker	125
1986	Greinton	Laffit Pincay, Jr.	122
1990	Ruhlmann	Gary Stevens	121

Jack Van Berg

Jack Van Berg, born June 7, 1936, in Columbus, Nebraska, is the winningest trainer in the history of thoroughbred racing, with 5,389 victories to his credit through 1989.

He's a son of Marion H. Van Berg, whose stable led the country's owners in wins 14 years (1952, 1955, 1956, a tie, and 1960–1970) and in money won 4 years (1965, 1968, 1969, and 1970). "I had the best teacher in the world, my father," said Jack, who went into the National Museum of Racing Hall of Fame in 1985, 15 years after his father was inducted. The elder Van Berg died in 1971, and Jack won the first running of the Marion H. Van Berg Memorial Stakes on July 8, 1972, at Ak-Sar-Ben with British Fleet, the last horse his father bred.

The hard-working Van Berg operates a stable that touches down in racing centers throughout America. He spends $30,000 a year on air fares, and his phone bill is about $5,000 a month. He has been the country's leading trainer in races won 9 times (1968–1970, 1972, 1974, 1976, 1983, 1984, and 1986) and in money won once (1976). He holds the record for most victories in a single year—496 in 1976. He won the Eclipse Award as the country's top trainer in 1984 and picked up his 5,000th career win on July 15, 1987, at Arlington Park with Art's Chandelle. His proteges include Billy Mott, Frank Brothers, Don Winfree, and Wayne Catalano.

Having seen his father succeed with problem horses, Van Berg utilized such equipment as earmuffs, blinkers, shadow roll, and a D-bit with a burr to straighten out the erratic Gate Dancer, whose victory in the 1984 Preakness was achieved in track-record time.

Van Berg lost 3 Breeders' Cup Classics by about 2 feet before triumphing in 1988 with Alysheba by a half-length. His Gate Dancer finished second in the 1984 Classic, a head behind Wild Again, but was disqualified to third; Gate Dancer lost the 1985 Classic by a head to Proud Truth, and Alysheba lost the 1987 Classic by a nose to Ferdinand. Alysheba was retired after the 1988 Classic with all-time record earnings of $6,679,242. Before a decision was reached on retiring the colt, Van Berg said he was "going to talk awfully hard in favor" of keeping him in competition another season. "Losing him would be like losing your leg," he said.

Alysheba was a popular runner, and after the 1988 Classic at Churchill Downs Van Berg said, "I don't know how many people they had here today, but they were all hollering for him. They had a sign out there, 'Alysheba For President!' He's got my vote, I can tell you that. He's done so much. He's traveled everywhere we've asked him to go—one end of the United States to the other—and he gives it his best effort every time." Indeed, during the course of his career, Alhsyeba won in 6 states and at 8 tracks. Following Alysheba's courageous win in the 1987 Kentucky Derby, when he stumbled badly and came close to going down in the homestretch after clipping heels with Bet Twice, Van Berg wept. After composing himself, he said, "I don't remember ever feeling this way before." Later, he said, "I had tears in my eyes after the race. And I lost my voice. First time in my life I was speechless."

Jack Van Berg's Career Wins

1957—10	1973—281
1958—16	1974—329
1959—16	1975—206
1960—27	1976—496
1961—16	1977—110
1962—19	1978—78
1963—21	1979—67
1964—124	1980—48
1965—146	1981—90
1966—116	1982—231
1967—187	1983—258
1968—256	1984—250
1969—239	1985—235
1970—282	1986—266
1971—190	1987—215
1972—287	1988—150
	1989—127

D. Wayne Lukas

D. Wayne Lukas, born September 2, 1935, in Antigo, Wisconsin, has an interesting background for a trainer. After graduating from the University of Wisconsin, he coached basketball for several years at Wisconsin high schools and served as an assistant basketball coach for 2 seasons back again at the University of Wisconsin.

Lukas trained 23 world champion quarter horses, including Dash for Cash, two-time Horse of the Year (1976–1977), and began training thoroughbreds full time in 1978. In his first dozen years with the thoroughbreds, he's accomplished great things. He's been the country's leading money-earning trainer for 7 straight years with

$4.2 million in 1983, $5.8 million in 1984, $11.1 million in 1985, $12.3 million in 1986, $17.5 million in 1987, $17.8 million in 1988, and $16.1 million in 1989. Moreover, he's won the Eclipse Award as the country's leading trainer in 1985, 1986, and 1987, and he's won a record 10 Breeders' Cup races, including 3 in 1988.

Many trainers go a lifetime without training a single champion, but already Lukas has had a record 12 in his care. Nine of Lukas' champions have been fillies—Althea, Family Style, Lady's Secret (1986 Horse of the Year, career winner in 25 of 45 races, and leading all-time money-earner among fillies and mares with $3,021,425), Landaluce, Life's Magic, North Sider, Open Mind, Sacahuista, and Winning Colors. His other 3 champions were Capote, 1986 Eclipse Award winner in the 2-year-old male division; Gulch, champion sprinter of 1988, and Steinlen, champion male turf horse of 1989.

A man with a sharp eye for yearlings, Lukas has enjoyed plenty of success at the horse auctions and at Keeneland alone has purchased 6 of the horses who went on to win championships—Capote, Family Style, Landaluce, Life's Magic, Sacahuista, and Winning Colors. He also bought Open Mind at public auction. At Keeneland's 1986 July Selected Yearling Sale, he bought Winning Colors for $575,000. Recalling his opinion of Winning Colors at the sale, Lukas said, "She had it all. When she walked out, I went around her about twice and I didn't want to draw a lot of attention. I said, 'Put her away.' It's like when Liz Taylor walks in a room. You don't have to have everybody tell you that's a pretty woman."

Lukas is the only trainer to saddle 2 fillies in the same Kentucky Derby (Life's Magic, 8th, and Althea, 19th, in 1984). He won the 1988 Derby with Winning Colors, only the third filly to triumph in the Churchill Downs classic.

His son, Jeff, oversees the stable's New York

division for most of the year. "His input and his contributions are paramount," Lukas said. "We're close, and we consider ourselves as one identity. Once I quit coaching, Jeff became more and more involved in the horse business because I became more and more involved in it."

Lukas gives Jeff credit for Winning Colors's success, saying: "He spent so much time [with her] that I became more of an adviser. Actually, all spring [in 1988] he more or less called the day-to-day shots. The minute we got on the victory stand [after the Kentucky Derby], the first thing I said is that the tragedy of the day was that Jeff elected to go back to the test barn with her and didn't share the moment, and yet he was probably the person most responsible for us all getting there."

D. Wayne Lukas' Winners in the Breeders' Cup

Year	Race	Winner	Jockey	Margin (lengths)
1985	Juvenile Fillies	Twilight Ridge	Jorge Velasquez	1
1985	Distaff	Life's Magic	Angel Cordero, Jr.	$6^1/4$
1986	Juvenile	Capote	Laffit Pincay, Jr.	$1^1/4$
1986	Distaff	Lady's Secret	Pat Day	$2^1/2$
1987	Distaff	Sacahuista	Randy Romero	$2^1/4$
1987	Juvenile	Success Express	José Santos	$1^3/4$
1988	Sprint	Gulch	Angel Cordero, Jr.	$^3/4$
1988	J. Fillies	Open Mind	Angel Cordero, Jr.	$1^3/4$
1988	Juvenile	Is It True	Laffit Pincay, Jr.	$1^1/4$
1989	Mile	Steinlen	José Santos	$^3/4$

Laz Barrera

Lazaro "Laz" Barrera, born May 8, 1924, in Havana, Cuba, was elected to the National Museum of Racing Hall of Fame in 1979 and is one of the most knowledgeable trainers in the sport. He was the leading money-winning trainer 4 years (1977–1980) and was honored with Eclipse Awards as the country's top trainer 4 straight years (1976-1979).

He has trained 2 Kentucky Derby winners— Bold Forbes (1976) and Affirmed (1978). Bold Forbes, a colt with great natural speed, was brought up to the Derby perfectly by Barrera. Instead of giving Bold Forbes workouts, the astute Barrera had the little colt gallop $1^1/2$ or 2 miles daily so that he could carry his speed a mile and a quarter. The front-running Bold Forbes covered the Derby's first 6 furlongs in $1:10^2/5$ and still had enough left to defeat the odds-on favorite, Honest Pleasure. On that same day, Barrera-trained horses won the Illinois Derby (Life's Hope) and the Carter Handicap (Due Diligence).

Besides Bold Forbes and Affirmed, Barrera has trained other champions: It's in the Air, J.O. Tobin, Lemhi Gold, and Tiffany Lass.

Barrera trained Affirmed to Horse of the Year titles in 1978 and 1979. "Affirmed is the best horse we've seen in our lifetimes," Barrera said.

Some people say the same thing about Laz Barrera as a trainer.

Shug McGaughey

Claude R. "Shug" McGaughey III, born January 6, 1951, in Lexington, Kentucky, was introduced to racing as a youth by his parents, who took him to Keeneland Race Course. "I liked the atmosphere and the feel of competition in the air," McGaughey said. "I was hooked."

McGaughey, who didn't come from a racing background, obtained his first trainer's license in 1979 and opened a public stable in 1980. On

November 11, 1985, he was named trainer for Ogden Phipps, and he brought that stable back to the prominence that it formerly had known. He trained Personal Ensign to a perfect lifetime record (13 for 13), the first horse since Colin (15 for 15 in 1907–1908) to retire unbeaten after a full career, and he won the 1989 Belmont Stakes with Easy Goer.

In 1988, he trained 8 Grade I winners from a stable of 37 horses, and he captured 15 Grade I stakes, 13 of them on the tough New York circuit. McGaughey was the leading percentage trainer in New York in 1987, 1988, and 1989 (100 or more starts) with 28 percent, 27 percent, and 30 percent, respectively. For his accomplishments in 1988, he was honored with the Eclipse Award as the country's leading trainer.

McGaughey sent out 5 starters on the 1988 Breeders' Cup championship card, including 3 favorites—Personal Ensign, who won the Distaff; Easy Goer, 2nd in the Juvenile; and Mining, 10th in the Sprint.

On August 5, 1989, he won 2 Grade I races on different fronts, Easy Goer capturing the Whitney Handicap at Saratoga and Awe Inspiring taking the American Derby at Arlington International Racecourse.

John Veitch

John Veitch, born June 27, 1945, in Lexington, Kentucky, grew up around horses. "I was virtually raised on C.V. Whitney's farm in Lexington," he said. Veitch attended Bradley University, majoring in history and international studies and playing halfback on the football team. He was inducted into Bradley's Hall of Fame in 1979.

He worked for his father, Hall of Fame trainer Sylvester Veitch, and then served a 3-year apprenticeship under another Hall of Fame trainer, Elliott Burch, at Rokeby Stable. He took out his first trainer's license in 1973 and in 1976 was

Trainer John Veitch

hired by Calumet Farm, remaining there until he resigned in 1982. "The first year was very dry," Veitch said, "but all the rest were good years for me and Calumet." Good years, indeed. Veitch trained Alydar and three champion fillies for Calumet—Our Mims (1977 champion 3-year-old filly), Davona Dale (1979 champion 3-year-old filly), and Before Dawn (1981 champion 2-year-old filly). Alydar is the only horse to finish second in all 3 Triple Crown races (1978).

Veitch went to work for John W. Galbreath and Darby Dan Farm in 1984 and won the Breeders' Cup Classic in 1985 with Proud Truth. "From the standpoint of an individual race, I would have to think that the Classic was as big a thrill as I've ever had," Veitch said. "It was wonderful, and certainly to win it for a man like Mr. Galbreath, who did so much in racing, it was a great thrill for him, and that made it even a greater thrill for me."

Galbreath, one of racing's greatest sportsmen, died in 1988 at the age of 90. "Mr. Galbreath's generation of owners was the last of a way of life—private stables, private farms, bred their own, raised their own, had their own trainers," Veitch said. "The Phippses, Mr. [Paul] Mellon, and now the Galbreath family—those are the last of the giants of the game, the people that made the game, actually. Those families invested great fortunes and great wealth for the benefit of the sport—not for themselves, but for the benefit of the sport."

Veitch won the 1988 Eclipse Award with Sunshine Forever as top male grass horse. He has started 4 horses in Gulfstream Park's premier race, the Florida Derby, and has won 3 times—Alydar (1978), Proud Truth (1985), and Brian's Time (1988). The other starter, Dr. Carter, finished 2nd in 1984.

He has sent out 5 horses in Breeders' Cup races, and 4 of them have brought home purse money—Proud Truth ($1,350,000, 1st in 1985 Classic), Sunshine Forever ($450,000, 2nd in 1988 Turf), Steal a Kiss ($108,000, 3rd in 1985 Juvenile Fillies), and Script Ohio ($70,000, 4th in 1984 Juvenile).

Neil Drysdale

Neil Drysdale, born December 11, 1947, in Sussex, England, is the son of a British cavalry officer. He studied at the University of Barcelona and taught English briefly. A trainer with a real talent with horses, Drysdale spent several years as Charlie Whittingham's assistant in California, where he learned the importance of "patience and planning."

He has trained many outstanding horses, including Princess Rooney (who won the 1984 Breeders' Cup Distaff), Tasso (the 1985 Breeders' Cup Juvenile victor), Prized (the 1989 Breeders' Cup Turf winner), and Bold 'n Determined (winner of 8 stakes in 1980). One of those victories for Bold 'n Determined was over Kentucky

Derby winner Genuine Risk in the Maskette.

Princess Rooney won the 1984 Distaff in a faster time for the mile and a quarter ($2:02^2/5$) than Wild Again did later on the card in the Classic ($2:03^2/5$). "It did cross my mind that she was so good at the time that I could have run her in the colt race [the Classic], because she just came up to the race so well," Drysdale said. "And I think probably if she had run in the colt race, there was a good possibility she would have won it. We aimed her specifically for the Breeders' Cup, and she cooperated nicely and just got better and better. That was, I think, probably one of the best races of her life, while I was training her."

Commenting on Bold 'n Determined, Drysdale said, "Wasn't she well-named?" In her nose win in the 1980 Maskette, Bold 'n Determined gave Genuine Risk 4 pounds (122-118). "We both came up to the race under the same circumstances— off a long layoff," Drysdale once recalled. "It was a genuine horse race. They hooked up at the head of the stretch and ran down the stretch together. It was a very exciting race. They had the whole stretch run to sort out their differences."

9

The Nine Best Racetracks in America

Keeneland should be the national park of racing. The beauty of spring with the clean, clear air and the blooms of the pears, crab apples, and dogwoods are excelled only in October by the yellows, golds, ambers, oranges, and reds of the same flora. If we could bottle April and October at Keeneland and sell it, we could instantly lower the national debt.

> Howard Battle,
> Keeneland racing secretary

Saratoga represents a reaffirmation of racing as enjoyment, of the original forces which first called it into being. You come away feeling that, well, there is going to be a good deal of concrete and gravel in your horoscope for a goodish while, but afterward there will be Saratoga again, with its shaded paddocks. . . .

> Joe Palmer, the greatest of all
> American turf writers

Racetracks, like people, have qualities of their own—personalities, if you will. Some are warm and friendly; others are cold and indifferent. Some take pride in their ambience; others are nothing more than concrete betting establishments. Some have style; others a conspicuous lack of it.

Join us as we take a look at some of America's racetracks with personality plus.

KEENELAND RACE COURSE, LEXINGTON, KENTUCKY

Beauty, as the saying goes, is in the eyes of the beholder. No matter what eyes gaze upon the Keeneland Race Course, however, it would be hard to award it anything but a perfect 10. Keeneland melts into nature to produce a postcard setting: the arbored drive, the manicured lawns, the tree-shaded saddling area, the ivy-covered walls, the Japanese yew in the infield that spells out "KEENELAND" in bushy greenery.

Located in the heart of Bluegrass country, 6 miles from Lexington, Kentucky, Keeneland was designed to be something special—a track that would cultivate an endearing appreciation and respect for the noble sport of horse racing. Keeneland was to provide an ambience that would cater to established horse lovers while simultaneously developing new horse-racing fans. Let other tracks instruct their public-address announcers to remind the fans to get their bets down. Let others run long seasons that are short on quality races. Let others do as they please. Keeneland leaders have preferred to do it their way, and have, since 1936.

"Racing as it was meant to be." That's Keeneland's slogan. And if you've ever been there, you know the significance of those words.

To this day, the motto continues to summarize the Keeneland philosophy as established by Hal Price Headley, one of the track's founders. "We

The horses charge down the stretch at Keeneland Race Course in Lexington, Kentucky. (Photo by Bill Straus, courtesy Keeneland Association)

want a place where those who love horses can come and picnic with us and thrill to the sport of the Bluegrass," he said in 1937. "We are not running a race plant to hear the click of the mutuel machines. We don't care whether the people who come here bet or not. If they want to bet, there is a place for them to do it. But we want them to come out here to enjoy God's sunshine, the fresh air, and to watch horses race."

Watch horses race. Not listen to the public-address announcer—Keeneland has never had one—but watch. Foregoing a public-address system is an attempt, says James E. "Ted" Bassett III, the Keeneland board chairman, "to emphasize the beauty of the horse, the pageantry, the tradition of racing—the emphasis being on the sporting aspects rather than the commercial."

Spring in Kentucky can mean only one thing: Derby fever. And early symptoms are sure to be apparent at Keeneland in the days that lead up to the Blue Grass Stakes, the top race of the season. An electricity fills the air as Derby contenders from around the country converge on Keeneland for the final important preparations prior to the Churchill Downs classic.

Aside from producing 14 horses from the Blue Grass that have gone on to win the Derby's first-place check, Keeneland was the site of a visit, on October 11, 1984, from Queen Elizabeth II, the only time she has ever been to races in the United States. Along the edge of the walking ring, the crowd stood 6 to 8 people deep in an effort to see the Queen. In the walking ring, the Queen met and shook hands with the jockeys who would ride in the featured Queen Elizabeth II Challenge Cup, along with Don Brumfield, Keeneland's all-time leading jockey whose mount had been withdrawn from the race.

Sintra won the feature, and afterward the crowd in the grandstand and clubhouse waited for the Queen to make her appearance in the winner's circle. Thousands were standing in anticipation, just as they would during the running of a race. During the presentation ceremony, cameras operated by professional photographers, as well as those belonging to amateurs in the stands, clicked with incredible rapidity. It's unlikely that any other single event in Keeneland's history has ever caused so many pictures to be taken.

The jockeys were overjoyed at meeting the Queen. Recalls Bobby Peck, the Keeneland clerk of scales, "She had something to say to every one of them. They were *really* impressed."

Later, Keeneland trustee Charles Nuckols, Jr., would remember the special afternoon. "Probably the most important race I ever saw at Keeneland was the first running of the Queen Elizabeth II Challenge Cup," he says. "It was special because of the Queen's presence and the prestige it brought to Keeneland."

SARATOGA RACE COURSE, SARATOGA SPRINGS, NEW YORK

Welcome to the graveyard. The Graveyard of Favorites, that is.

You don't have to be a student of racing history to know that many a champion has gone down to a stunning defeat at Saratoga, the ancient track located in upstate New York. If you've just casually followed the sport in recent years, you remember such notables as Secretariat, Conquistador Cielo, and Manila losing as heavy favorites at Saratoga.

Secretariat, the superhorse who swept the 1973 Triple Crown, went to the post in that summer's Whitney Stakes as an overwhelming favorite; he came home a loser to Onion. Conquistador Cielo, who was voted Horse of the Year in 1982, finished third as the 2-5 favorite in the Travers that season, snapping a 7-race winning streak. The great grass runner Manila won 10 of his last 11 career starts,

Queen Elizabeth II meets
the jockeys in the
inaugural running of the
Queen Elizabeth II
Challenge Cup. (Photo by
Bill Straus, courtesy
Keeneland Association)

the lone defeat coming at 3-10 odds in the 1987 Bernard Baruch.

There have been many other upsets at Saratoga, but when it comes to firmly establishing this ancient track as the graveyard of all graveyards for favorites, it does take some leafing back through the pages of racing history to find a pair of races that provided 2 of the greatest upsets in the annals of the sport.

First, there was the 1919 Sanford Memorial Stakes, the only race that the legendary Man o' War ever lost. His conqueror? The aptly named Upset.

And then there was the 1930 Travers, the only loss that Gallant Fox, that season's Triple Crown champion, suffered in 10 starts as a 3-year-old. Not only did he lose, but he struggled home a full 6 or 8 lengths in sticky mud behind a 100-1 longshot by the name of Jim Dandy.

The great Joe Palmer once wrote that Saratoga wears tradition lightly "because it is a graceful, irresponsible, gay tradition, and its ghosts are pleasant ghosts."

The bluebloods—horses and people alike—converge on Saratoga for its summer meeting. For years, Saratoga Race Course in August simply has been *the* place to be for all of the establishment people in racing.

In greeting an influx of racegoers, Saratoga Springs, New York, offers more than just horse racing. There's ballet and music, museums and art, fine dining and magnificent Victorian houses. A city with a fascinating history, Saratoga Springs was once a famous gambling resort that attracted high rollers such as John "Bet a Million" Gates.

The Travers, for 3-year-olds, is Saratoga's top-drawer race. Known as the "Midsummer Derby," it has been won by such stars as Twenty Grand (1931), Granville (1936), Whirlaway (1941), Shut Out (1942), Native Dancer (1953), Gallant Man (1957), Sword Dancer (1959), Jaipur (1962),

They're off and running at Saratoga. (New York Racing Association Photo)

Buckpasser (1966), Damascus (1967), Arts and Letters (1969), Wajima (1975), Alydar (1978, on disqualification), Temperence Hill (1980), Play Fellow (1983), Chief's Crown (1985), Java Gold (1987), and Easy Goer (1989). For decades, a canoe drifted in Saratoga's infield lake, and in 1962 the tradition was started of painting it in the colors of the Travers winner.

Pervaded by a country-fair atmosphere, Saratoga is a fun place to attend the races. Many fans love to spend the afternoon in a picnic and recreation area—complete with television monitors and a betting pavilion—behind the grandstand.

ARLINGTON INTERNATIONAL RACECOURSE, ARLINGTON HEIGHTS, ILLINOIS

Arlington International Racecourse is unique in the truest sense of the word: one of a kind.

Trainer Cheryl Kolbrick had a horse entered on June 28, 1989, at Arlington International Racecourse, the reopening of the track. "When I walked in, I felt like maybe I ought to take off my shoes and go in my stocking feet," she says. "It's gorgeous. It is a showplace."

Track owner Richard L. Duchossois spared no expense in rebuilding Arlington. A devastating fire leveled the grandstand and clubhouse in 1985, yet just 25 days later the Budweiser-Arlington Million was run . . . after the demolition and removal of the burned-out stands and the erection of tents and bleachers. The race that year was appropriately called the "Miracle Million."

There's no better place to watch the races than Arlington, an elegant 6-story structure. Vertical supports don't exist, meaning that no seats in the clubhouse and grandstand are blocked by support beams.

"This is the most beautiful racetrack I've ever seen in my life," says veteran jockey Jorge Velasquez. "It's out of this world. This is *it*. This is gorgeous."

CHURCHILL DOWNS, LOUISVILLE, KENTUCKY

Churchill Downs has been the site of the world-famous Kentucky Derby since 1875. Col. M. Lewis Clark founded the Derby and served as its track president for the first 20 runnings of the race. He laid the foundation for the Derby, and Col. Matt J. Winn, a great promoter, came along early in the century to rejuvenate the race, which had fallen on hard times. Col. Winn, who built the Derby into "the greatest 2 minutes in sports," remained at the Downs until his death in 1949. He saw all of the first 75 runnings of the Derby.

The Derby draws worldwide interest and has attracted more than 100,000 fans annually since 1969, the last year of Southern gentleman Wathen Knebelkamp's reign as track president. He was succeeded by Lynn Stone, track president until Tom Meeker took over in the late summer of 1984. Under aggressive leadership, the Downs has changed its image while still retaining its old charm. Famed for the twin spires that have stood atop the stands since 1895, the Downs served as host track for the 1988 Breeders' Cup, drawing a record crowd of 71,237.

GULFSTREAM PARK, HALLANDALE, FLORIDA

Gulfstream Park is Florida's premier racetrack. Located close to the Atlantic Ocean, Gulfstream was host to the 1989 Breeders' Cup championship card attracting a state-record crowd of 51,342.

For years, Gulfstream has had a reputation as an important prepping ground for the Triple Crown classics. The Florida Derby, the showcase race of the Gulfstream meeting, has served as a launching pad for 14 horses who have gone on to win the Kentucky Derby, 15 who have triumphed in the Preakness, and 10 who have captured the Belmont. That adds up to a total of 39 winners of Triple Crown races coming from the "Run for the Orchids," which was inaugurated at Gulfstream in 1952.

In 3 of its runnings, the Florida Derby has produced 6 of the Triple Crown's 9 in-the-money finishers (1960, 1964, and 1987).

Why is it that Gulfstream Park is *the* place to be with a good 3-year-old leading up to the spring classics?

"Probably the best thing we have going for us is the weather," said Tommy Trotter, the Gulfstream director of racing and racing secretary. "In training up to the Triple Crown, Florida's weather during that time is hard to beat. We have no problem with too much rain or anything like that. When bringing a 3-year-old into the Triple Crown, you want to go into an area where you feel like you can plan and have a good deal of satisfaction in knowing that the weather is in your favor."

Besides horse racing, Florida Derby Day offers plenty of other entertainment. Billed as "The Greatest Show on Turf," the day features such attractions as the Florida State University Flying High Circus, water skiers, and marching bands. The traditional "Wild Animal Race" is now extinct on Florida Derby Day. Held from 1960 through 1989, the race attracted all kinds of animals, including elephants, bears, reindeer, Bengal tigers, and camels.

Just as the mint julep is the drink of the day at Churchill Downs on the first Saturday in May, the Captain Morgan Derby Daiquiri is the featured drink of the Florida Derby.

SANTA ANITA PARK, ARCADIA, CALIFORNIA

Located close to the San Gabriel Mountains, Santa Anita Park is known as "The Great Race Place," a description that fits this track perfectly. Santa Anita simply is 1 of the great racetracks of the world. The facility itself is beautiful, and the racing there just can't be beaten.

Many of the best jockeys in America compete at Santa Anita, including Laffit Pincay, Jr., Chris McCarron, Eddie Delahoussaye, and Pat Valenzuela. Bill Shoemaker was a Santa Anita veteran before his retirement in 1990. Such trainers as Charlie Whittingham, D. Wayne Lukas, and Laz Barrera are Santa Anita regulars.

The track offers outstanding purses and in turn attracts the finest of horses. The highlight race is the Santa Anita Handicap, which was inaugurated in 1935. Another attractive race is the Santa Anita Derby for 3-year-olds. Four straight Kentucky Derby winners—Ferdinand (1986), Alysheba (1987), Winning Colors (1988), and Sunday Silence (1989)—raced at Santa Anita as 3-year-olds before heading to Louisville for the Run for the Roses.

BELMONT PARK, ELMONT, NEW YORK

Belmont Park, which had its inaugural meeting in 1905, is a huge track with a $1^1/2$-mile dirt oval and two grass courses inside it. Some of racing's most famous owners—Odgen Phipps, Darby Dan Farm, and Rokeby Stable—traditionally stable at Belmont.

Many of the best horses in American racing history have raced at Belmont, including the following, who made their career debuts there: Affirmed, Colin, Count Fleet, Man o' War, Nashua, Ruffian, and Seattle Slew.

In 1971, the second largest crowd in New York sports history—82,694—attended the

Belmont Stakes to watch Canonero II in his unsuccessful bid to win the Triple Crown.

REMINGTON PARK, OKLAHOMA CITY, OKLAHOMA

Remington Park, a $97 million facility which opened in 1988, was the first track in the world to conduct racing on Equitrack, an all-weather surface made up of natural Oklahoma soil which uses a polymer coating as a binding agent, thus ensuring faster and better drainage capability. "Equitrack will revolutionize racing," says Hall of Fame trainer Jack Van Berg.

Remington has more going for it than Equitrack. It has a grand facility, a top staff, and a bright, bright future.

DEL MAR RACE TRACK, DEL MAR, CALIFORNIA

Located near San Diego, California, Del Mar is the track where the turf meets the surf. Founded by Bing Crosby and Pat O'Brien, Del Mar has plenty to offer its patrons—a first-rate facility and top-class racing. Del Mar, which hosted its 50th season of thoroughbred racing in 1989, has made tremendous growth in attendance, betting, and purses over the past two decades.

If you are fortunate enough to live near one of these tracks, or even near one of the smaller tracks around the country, take advantage of that proximity and go watch the horses. The experience is invaluable in becoming a successful bettor.

Award Winners

NATIONAL MUSEUM OF RACING HALL OF FAME

Horses (year elected and year foaled)

Ack Ack (1986, 1966)
Affectionately (1989, 1960)
Affirmed (1980, 1975)
Alsab (1976, 1939)
Alydar (1989, 1975)
American Eclipse (1970, 1814)
Armed (1963, 1941)
Artful (1956, 1902)
Assault (1964, 1943)
Battleship (1969, 1927)
Bed o' Roses (1976, 1947)
Beldame (1956, 1901)
Ben Brush (1955, 1893)
Bewitch (1977, 1945)
Black Gold (1989, 1921)
Blue Larkspur (1957, 1926)
Bold Ruler (1973, 1954)
Bon Nouvel (1976, 1960)
Boston (1955, 1833)
Broomstick (1956, 1901)
Buckpasser (1970, 1963)
Busher (1964, 1942)
Bushranger (1967, 1930)
Cafe Prince (1985, 1970)
Carry Back (1975, 1958)
Challedon (1977, 1936)
Chris Evert (1988, 1971)
Cicada (1967, 1959)
Citation (1959, 1945)
Coaltown (1983, 1945)
Colin (1956, 1905)

Commando (1956, 1898)
Count Fleet (1961, 1940)
Dahlia (1981, 1970)
Damascus (1974, 1964)
Dark Mirage (1974, 1965)
Davona Dale (1985, 1976)
Desert Vixen (1979, 1970)
Devil Diver (1980, 1939)
Discovery (1969, 1931)
Domino (1955, 1891)
Dr. Fager (1971, 1964)
Elkridge (1966, 1938)
Emperor of Norfolk (1988, 1885)
Equipoise (1957, 1928)
Exterminator (1957, 1915)
Fairmount (1985, 1921)
Fair Play (1956, 1905)
Fashion (1980, 1837)
Firenze (1981, 1884)
Forego (1979, 1970)
Gallant Bloom (1977, 1966)
Gallant Fox (1957, 1927)
Gallant Man (1987, 1954)
Gallorette (1962, 1942)
Gamely (1980, 1964)
Genuine Risk (1986, 1977)
Good and Plenty (1956, 1900)
Grey Lag (1957, 1918)
Hamburg (1986, 1895)
Hanover (1955, 1884)
Henry of Navarre (1985, 1891)
Hindoo (1955, 1878)
Imp (1965, 1894)
Jay Trump (1971, 1957)
Jolly Roger (1955, 1922)
Kelso (1967, 1957)
Kentucky (1983, 1861)
Kingston (1955, 1884)
L'Escargot (1977, 1963)
Lexington (1955, 1850)
Longfellow (1971, 1867)

Luke Blackburn (1956, 1877)
Majestic Prince (1988, 1966)
Man o' War (1957, 1917)
Miss Woodford (1967, 1880)
Myrtlewood (1979, 1932)
Nashua (1965, 1952)
Native Dancer (1963, 1950)
Native Diver (1978, 1959)
Neji (1966, 1950)
Northern Dancer (1976, 1961)
Oedipus (1978, 1946)
Old Rosebud (1968, 1911)
Omaha (1965, 1932)
Pan Zareta (1972, 1910)
Parole (1984, 1879)
Peter Pan (1956, 1904)
Princess Doreen (1982, 1921)
Real Delight (1987, 1949)
Regret (1957, 1912)
Reigh Count (1978, 1925)
Roamer (1981, 1911)
Roseben (1956, 1901)
Round Table (1972, 1954)
Ruffian (1976, 1972)
Ruthless (1975, 1864)
Salvator (1955, 1886)
Sarazen (1957, 1921)
Seabiscuit (1958, 1933)
Searching (1978, 1952)
Seattle Slew (1981, 1974)
Secretariat (1974, 1970)
Shuvee (1975, 1966)
Silver Spoon (1978, 1956)
Sir Archy (1955, 1805)
Sir Barton (1957, 1916)
Spectacular Bid (1982, 1976)
Stymie (1975, 1941)
Susan's Girl (1976, 1969)
Swaps (1966, 1952)
Sword Dancer (1977, 1956)
Sysonby (1956, 1902)

Ten Broeck (1982, 1872)
Tim Tam (1985, 1955)
Tom Fool (1960, 1949)
Top Flight (1966, 1929)
Tosmah (1984, 1961)
Twenty Grand (1957, 1928)
Twilight Tear (1963, 1941)
Two Lea (1982, 1946)
War Admiral (1958, 1934)
Whirlaway (1959, 1938)
Whisk Broom II (1979, 1907)
Zev (1983, 1920)

Trainers (year elected)

Lazaro S. Barrera (1979)
H. Guy Bedwell (1971)
Edward D. Brown (1984)
J. Elliott Burch (1980)
Preston M. Burch (1963)
William P. Burch (1955)
Fred Burlew (1973)
J. Dallett Byers (1967)
Frank E. Childs (1968)
Henry S. Clark (1982)
W. Burling Cocks (1985)
William Duke (1956)
Louis Feustel (1964)
James Fitzsimmons (1958)
John M. Gaver, Sr. (1966)
Thomas J. Healey (1955)
Samuel C. Hildreth (1955)
Maximiliam Hirsch (1959)
William J. Hirsch (1982)
Thomas Hitchcock (1973)
Hollie Hughes (1973)
John J. Hyland (1956)
Hirsch Jacobs (1958)
H. Allen Jerkens (1975)
William R. Johnson (1986)
LeRoy Jolley (1987)
Benjamin A. Jones (1958)

Horace A. Jones (1959)
A. Jack Joyner (1955)
Lucien Laurin (1977)
J. Howard Lewis (1969)
Horatio A. Luro (1980)
John E. Madden (1983)
Jim Maloney (1989)
. Frank Martin (1981)
Henry McDaniel (1956)
MacKenzie Miller (1987)
William Molter (1960)
W. F. Mulholland (1967)
Edward A. Neloy (1983)
John A. Nerud (1972)
Burley Parke (1986)
Angel Penna (1988)
Jacob Pincus (1988)
John W. Rogers (1955)
James G. Rowe, Sr. (1955)
Robert A. Smith (1976)
D. M. Smithwick (1971)
W. C. "Woody" Stephens (1976)
Henry J. Thompson (1969)
Harry Trotsek (1984)
Jack Van Berg (1985)
Marion Van Berg (1970)
Sylvester Veitch (1977)
R. W. Walden (1970)
Sherrill W. Ward (1978)
Frank Whiteley, Jr. (1978)
Charles Whittingham (1974)
G. Carey Winfrey (1975)
William C. Winfrey (1971)

Jockeys (year elected)

Frank "Dooley" Adams (1970)
John Adams (1965)
Joe Aitcheson, Jr. (1978)
G. Edward Arcaro (1958)
Ted F. Atkinson (1957)
Braulio Baeza (1976)

Carroll K. Bassett (1972)
Walter Blum (1987)
George Bostwick (1968)
Sam Boulmetis, Sr. (1973)
Steve Brooks (1963)
Thomas H. Burns (1983)
James H. Butwell (1984)
Frank Coltiletti (1970)
Angel Cordero, Jr. (1988)
Robert "Specs" Crawford (1973)
Lavelle "Buddy" Ensor (1962)
Laverne Fator (1955)
Mack Garner (1969)
Edward Garrison (1955)
Avelino Gomez (1982)
Henry F. Griffin (1956)
O. Eric Guerin (1972)
William J. Hartack (1959)
Albert Johnson (1971)
William J. Knapp (1969)
Clarence Kummer (1972)
Charles Kurtsinger (1967)
John P. Loftus (1959)
John Eric Longden (1958)
Daniel A. Maher (1955)
J. Linus "Pony" McAtee (1956)
Chris McCarron (1989)
Conn McCreary (1975)
Rigan McKinney (1968)
James McLaughlin (1955)
Walter Miller (1955)
Isaac B. Murphy (1955)
Ralph Neves (1960)
Joe Notter (1963)
George M. Odom (1955)
Winfield O'Connor (1956)
Frank O'Neill (1956)
Ivan H. Parke (1978)
Gilbert W. Patrick (1970)
Laffit Pincay, Jr. (1975)
Samuel Purdy (1970)

John Reiff (1970)
Alfred Robertson (1971)
John L. Rotz (1983)
Earl Sande (1955)
Carroll H. Shilling (1970)
William Shoemaker (1958)
Willie Simms (1977)
Tod Sloan (1955)
Alfred P. Smithwick (1973)
James Stout (1968)
Fred Taral (1955)
Bayard Tuckerman, Jr. (1973)
Ron Turcotte (1979)
Nash Turner (1955)
Robert N. Ussery (1980)
George M. Woolf (1955)
Raymond Workman (1956)
Manuel Ycaza (1977)

ECLIPSE AWARD WINNERS (1971–1989)

The *Daily Racing Form*, the National Turf Writers Association and the Thoroughbred Racing Associations formed the Eclipse Awards in 1971.

Horse of the Year

1971	Ack Ack (age 5)	1981	John Henry (6)
1972	Secretariat (2)	1982	Conquistador Cielo (3)
1973	Secretariat (3)		
1974	Forego (4)	1983	All Along (4)
1975	Forego (5)	1984	John Henry (9)
1976	Forego (6)	1985	Spend a Buck (3)
1977	Seattle Slew (3)	1986	Lady's Secret (4)
1978	Affirmed (3)	1987	Ferdinand (4)
1979	Affirmed (4)	1988	Alysheba (4)
1980	Spectacular Bid (4)	1989	Sunday Silence (3)

Older Colt, Horse, or Gelding

1971 Ack Ack (age 5)	1981 John Henry (6)
1972 Autobiography (4)	1982 Lemhi Gold (4)
1973 Riva Ridge (4)	1983 Bates Motel (4)
1974 Forego (4)	1984 Slew o' Gold (4)
1975 Forego (5)	1985 Vanlandingham (4)
1976 Forego (6)	1986 Turkoman (4)
1977 Forego (7)	1987 Ferdinand (4)
1978 Seattle Slew (4)	1988 Alysheba (4)
1979 Affirmed (4)	1989 Blushing John (4)
1980 Spectacular Bid (4)	

Older Filly or Mare

1971 Shuvee (age 5)	1981 Relaxing (5)
1972 Typecast (6)	1982 Track Robbery (6)
1973 Susan's Girl (4)	1983 Ambassador of Luck (4)
1974 Desert Vixen (4)	
1975 Susan's Girl (6)	1984 Princess Rooney (4)
1976 Proud Delta (4)	1985 Life's Magic (4)
1977 Cascapedia (4)	1986 Lady's Secret (4)
1978 Late Bloomer (4)	1987 North Sider (5)
1979 Waya (5)	1988 Personal Ensign (4)
1980 Glorious Song (4)	1989 Bayakoa (5)

3-Year-Old Filly

1971 Turkish Trousers	1981 Wayward Lass
1972 Susan's Girl	1982 Christmas Past
1973 Desert Vixen	1983 Heartlight No. One
1974 Chris Evert	1984 Life's Magic
1975 Ruffian	1985 Mom's Command
1976 Revidere	1986 Tiffany Lass
1977 Our Mims	1987 Sacahuista
1978 Tempest Queen	1988 Winning Colors
1979 Davona Dale	1989 Open Mind
1980 Genuine Risk	

3-Year-Old Colt

1971	Canonero II	1981	Pleasant Colony
1972	Key to the Mint	1982	Conquistador
1973	Secretariat		Cielo
1974	Little Current	1983	Slew o' Gold
1975	Wajima	1984	Swale
1976	Bold Forbes	1985	Spend a Buck
1977	Seattle Slew	1986	Snow Chief
1978	Affirmed	1987	Alysheba
1979	Spectacular Bid	1988	Risen Star
1980	Temperence Hill	1989	Sunday Silence

2-Year-Old Filly

1971	Numbered	1980	Heavenly Cause
	Account	1981	Before Dawn
1972	La Prevoyante	1982	Landaluce
1973	Talking Picture	1983	Althea
1974	Ruffian	1984	Outstandingly
1975	Dearly Precious	1985	Family Style
1976	Sensational	1986	Brave Raj
1977	Lakeville Miss	1987	Epitome
1978	Tie: Candy Eclair,	1988	Open Mind
	It's in the Air	1989	Go for Wand
1979	Smart Angle		

2-Year-Old Colt

1971	Riva Ridge	1981	Deputy Minister
1972	Secretariat	1982	Roving Boy
1973	Protagonist	1983	Devil's Bag
1974	Foolish Pleasure	1984	Chief's Crown
1975	Honest Pleasure	1985	Tasso
1976	Seattle Slew	1986	Capote
1977	Affirmed	1987	Forty Niner
1978	Spectacular Bid	1988	Easy Goer
1979	Rockhill Native	1989	Rhythm
1980	Lord Avie		

Champion Turf Horse

1971 Run the Gantlet (age 3)	1975 Snow Knight (4)
	1976 Youth (3)
1972 Cougar II (6)	1977 Johnny D. (3)
1973 Secretariat (3)	1978 Mac Diarmida (3)
1974 Dahlia (4)	

Champion Female Turf Horse

1979 Trillion (age 5)	1985 Pebbles (4)
1980 Just A Game II (4)	1986 Estrapade (6)
1981 De La Rose (3)	1987 Miesque (3)
1982 April Run (4)	1988 Miesque (4)
1983 All Along (4)	1989 Brown Bess (7)
1984 Royal Heroine (4)	

Champion Male Turf Horse

1979 Bowl Game (age 5)	1985 Cozzene (4)
	1986 Manila (3)
1980 John Henry (5)	1987 Theatrical (5)
1981 John Henry (6)	1988 Sunshine Forever (3)
1982 Perrault (5)	
1983 John Henry (8)	1989 Steinlen (6)
1984 John Henry (9)	

Sprinter

1971 Ack Ack (age 5)	1981 Guilty Conscience (5)
1972 Chou Croute (4)	
1973 Shecky Greene (3	1982 Gold Beauty (3)
1974 Forego (4)	1983 Chinook Pass (4)
1975 Gallant Bob (3)	1984 Eillo (4)
1976 My Juliet (4)	1985 Precisionist (4)
1977 What a Summer (4)	1986 Smile (4)
1978 Tie: Dr. Patches (4)	1987 Groovy (4)
J. O. Tobin (4)	1988 Gulch (4)
1979 Star de Naskra (4)	1989 Safety Kept (3)
1980 Plugged Nickle (3)	

Special Award

1971	Robert J. Kleberg	1984	C. V. Whitney
1974	Charles Hatton	1985	Arlington Park
1976	Bill Shoemaker	1987	Anheuser-Busch
1980	John T. Landry	1988	Edward J.
	Pierre E. Bellocq		DeBartolo, Sr.
	(Peb)		

Outstanding Trainer

1971	Charles Whittingham	1982	Charles Whittingham
1972	Lucien Laurin	1983	W. C. "Woody" Stephens
1973	H. Allen Jerkens	1984	Jack Van Berg
1974	Sherrill Ward	1985	D. Wayne Lukas
1975	Steve DiMauro	1986	D. Wayne Lukas
1976	Lazaro Barrera	1987	D. Wayne Lukas
1977	Lazaro Barrera	1988	Claude "Shug" McGaughey
1978	Lazaro Barrera	1989	Charles Whittingham
1979	Lazaro Barrera		
1980	Grover "Bud" Delp		
1981	Ron McAnally		

Steeplechase or Hurdle Horse

1971	Shadow Brook (age 7)	1980	Zaccio (4)
1972	Soothsayer (5)	1981	Zaccio (5)
1973	Athenian Idol (5)	1982	Zaccio (6)
1974	Gran Kan (8)	1983	Flatterer (4)
1975	Life's Illusion (4)	1984	Flatterer (5)
1976	Straight and True (6)	1985	Flatterer (6)
1977	Cafe Prince (7)	1986	Flatterer (7)
1978	Cafe Prince (8)	1987	Inlander (6)
1979	Martie's Anger (4)	1988	Jimmy Lorenzo (6)
		1989	Highland Bud (4)

Outstanding Jockey

1971	Laffit Pincay, Jr.	1981	Bill Shoemaker
1972	Braulio Baeza	1982	Angel Cordero, Jr.
1973	Laffit Pincay, Jr.	1983	Angel Cordero, Jr.
1974	Laffit Pincay, Jr.	1984	Pat Day
1975	Braulio Baeza	1985	Laffit Pincay, Jr.
1976	Sandy Hawley	1986	Pat Day
1977	Steve Cauthen	1987	Pat Day
1978	Darrel McHargue	1988	José Santos
1979	Laffit Pincay, Jr.	1989	Kent Desormeaux
1980	Chris McCarron		

Outstanding Owner

1971	Mr. and Mrs. E. E. Fogelson	1982	Viola Sommer
		1983	John Franks
1974	Dan Lasater	1984	John Franks
1975	Dan Lasater	1985	Mr. and Mrs. Eugene Klein
1976	Dan Lasater		
1977	Maxwell Gluck	1986	Mr. and Mrs. Eugene Klein
1978	Harbor View Farm		
1979	Harbor View Farm	1987	Mr. and Mrs. Eugene Klein
1980	Mr. and Mrs. Bertram Firestone		
		1988	Ogden Phipps
1981	Dotsam Stable	1989	Ogden Phipps

Outstanding Apprentice Jockey

1971	Gene St. Leon	1981	Richard Migliore
1972	Thomas Wallis	1982	Alberto Delgado
1973	Steve Valdez	1983	Declan Murphy
1974	Chris McCarron	1984	Wesley Ward
1975	Jimmy Edwards	1985	Art Madrid, Jr.
1976	George Martens	1986	Allen Stacy
1977	Steve Cauthen	1987	Kent Desormeaux
1978	Ronnie Franklin	1988	Steve Capanas
1979	Cash Asmussen	1989	Michael Luzzi
1980	Frank Lovato, Jr.		

Award of Merit

1976	Jack J. Dreyfus	1981	Bill Shoemaker
1977	Steve Cauthen	1984	John Gaines
1978	Ogden Mills "Dinny" Phipps	1985	Keene Daingerfield
		1986	Herman Cohen
1979	Frank E. "Jimmy" Kilroe	1987	J. B. Faulconer
		1988	John Forsythe
1980	John D. Schapiro	1989	Michael P. Sandler

Man of the Year

1972	John W. Galbreath	1974	William McKnight
1973	Edward P. Taylor	1975	John A. Morris

Outstanding Owner-Breeeder

1971 Paul Mellon
1972 Meadow Stable/Meadow Stud (C. T. Chenery)
1973 Meadow Stable/Meadow Stud (C. T. Chenery)

Outstanding Breeder

1974	John W. Galbreath	1982	Fred W. Hooper
1975	Fred W. Hooper	1983	Edward P. Taylor
1976	Nelson Bunker Hunt	1984	Claiborne Farm
		1985	Nelson Bunker Hunt
1977	Edward P. Taylor		
1978	Harbor View Farm	1986	Paul Mellon
1979	Claiborne Farm	1987	Nelson Bunker Hunt
1980	Mrs. Henry D. Paxson		
		1988	Ogden Phipps
1981	Golden Chance Farm	1989	North Ridge Farm

Outstanding Achievement

971 Charles Engelhard (posthumously)
972 Arthur B. Hancock, Jr. (posthumously)

TRIPLE CROWN WINNERS
(Kentucky Derby, Preakness, Belmont)

Year	Horse	Owner
1919	Sir Barton	J.K.L. Ross
1930	Gallant Fox	Belair Stud
1935	Omaha	Belair Stud
1937	War Admiral	Glen Riddle Farm
1941	Whirlaway	Calumet Farm
1943	Count Fleet	Mrs. John D. He
1946	Assault	King Ranch
1948	Citation	Calumet Farm
1973	Secretariat	Meadow Stable
1977	Seattle Slew	*Karen Taylor
1978	Affirmed	Harbor View Fa

* Seattle Slew ran in Karen Taylor's name but actually was owned by Mrs. Taylor and her husband, Mickey, along with Dr. and Mrs. Jim Hill.

Triple Crown notes

• Gallant Fox is the only Triple Crown winner to sire a Triple Crown winner—Omaha (1935).

• Gallant Fox and Omaha both were foaled at Claiborne Farm, near Paris, Kentucky.

• Whirlaway and Citation both were foaled at Calumet Farm, Lexington, Kentucky.

KENTUCKY DERBY WINNERS

Year	Horse	Jockey
1875	Aristides	O. Lewis
1876	Vagrant	R. Swim
1877	Baden-Baden	W. Walker
1878	Day Star	J. Carter
1879	Lord Murphy	C. Shauer
1880	Fonso	G. Lewis
1881	Hindoo	J. McLaughlin

Trainer	Jockey
H. Guy Bedwell	Johnny Loftus
Jim Fitzsimmons	Earl Sande
Jim Fitzsimmons	William Saunders
George Conway	Charley Kurtsinger
Ben A. Jones	Eddie Arcaro
Don Cameron	Johnny Longden
Max Hirsch	Warren Mehrtens
H.A. "Jimmy" Jones	Eddie Arcaro
and Ben A. Jones	
Lucien Laurin	Ron Turcotte
Billy Turner	Jean Cruguet
Laz Barrera	Steve Cauthen

• Eight of the Triple Crown winners were foaled in Kentucky. The exceptions: Assault (Texas), Secretariat (Virginia), and Affirmed (Florida).

• Steve Cauthen, 18, was the youngest jockey to win the Triple Crown.

• Sir Barton was a maiden before he won the Kentucky Derby.

Year	Horse	Jockey
1882	Apollo	B. Hurd
1883	Leonatus	W. Donohue
1884	Buchanan	I. Murphy
1885	Joe Cotton	E. Henderson
1886	Ben Ali	P. Duffy
1887	Montrose	I. Lewis
1888	Macbeth II	G. Covington
1889	Spokane	T. Kiley
1890	Riley	I. Murphy

KENTUCKY DERBY WINNERS
(continued)

Year	Horse	Jockey
1891	Kingman	I. Murphy
1892	Azra	A. Clayton
1893	Lookout	E. Kunze
1894	Chant	F. Goodale
1895	Halma	J. Perkins
1896	Ben Brush	W. Simms
1897	Typhoon II	F. Garner
1898	Plaudit	W. Simms
1899	Manuel	F. Taral
1900	Lieut. Gibson	J. Boland
1901	His Eminence	J. Winkfield
1902	Alan-a-Dale	J. Winkfield
1903	Judges Himes	H. Booker
1904	Elwood	F. Prior
1905	Agile	J. Martin
1906	Sir Huon	R. Troxler
1907	Pink Star	A. Minder
1908	Stone Street	A. Pickens
1909	Wintergreen	V. Powers
1910	Donau	F. Herbert
1911	Meridian	G. Archibald
1912	Worth	C.H. Shilling
1913	Donerail	R. Goose
1914	Old Rosebud	J. McCabe
1915	Regret	J. Notter
1916	George Smith	J. Loftus
1917	Omar Khayyam	C. Borel
1918	Exterminator	W. Knapp
1919	Sir Barton	J. Loftus
1920	Paul Jones	T. Rice
1921	Behave Yourself	C. Thompson
1922	Morvich	A. Johnson
1923	Zev	E. Sande
1924	Black Gold	J.D. Mooney
1925	Flying Ebony	E. Sande
1926	Bubbling Over	A. Johnson
1927	Whiskery	L. McAtee

Year	Horse	Jockey
1928	Reigh Count	C. Lang
1929	Clyde Van Dusen	L. McAtee
1930	Gallant Fox	E. Sande
1931	Twenty Grand	C. Kurtsinger
1932	Burgoo King	E. James
1933	Brokers Tip	D. Meade
1934	Cavalcade	M. Garner
1935	Omaha	W. Saunders
1936	Bold Venture	I. Hanford
1937	War Admiral	C. Kurtsinger
1938	Lawrin	E. Arcaro
1939	Johnstown	J. Stout
1940	Gallahadion	C. Bierman
1941	Whirlaway	E. Arcaro
1942	Shut Out	W.D. Wright
1943	Count Fleet	J. Longden
1944	Pensive	C. McCreary
1945	Hoop Jr.	E. Arcaro
1946	Assault	W. Mehrtens
1947	Jet Pilot	E. Guerin
1948	Citation	E. Arcaro
1949	Ponder	S. Brooks
1950	Middleground	W. Boland
1951	Count Turf	C. McCreary
1952	Hill Gail	E. Arcaro
1953	Dark Star	H. Moreno
1954	Determine	R. York
1955	Swaps	W. Shoemaker
1956	Needles	D. Erb
1957	Iron Liege	W. Hartack
1958	Tim Tam	I. Valenzuela
1959	Tomy Lee	W. Shoemaker
1960	Venetian Way	W. Hartack
1961	Carry Back	J. Sellers
1962	Decidedly	W. Hartack
1963	Chateauguay	B. Baeza
1964	Northern Dancer	W. Hartack
1965	Lucky Debonair	W. Shoemaker
1966	Kauai King	D. Brumfield
1967	Proud Clarion	R. Ussery

KENTUCKY DERBY WINNERS
(continued)

Year	Horse	Jockey
1968	Forward Pass	I. Valenzuela
1969	Majestic Prince	W. Hartack
1970	Dust Commander	M. Manganello
1971	Canonero II	G. Avila
1972	Riva Ridge	R. Turcotte
1973	Secretariat	R. Turcotte
1974	Cannonade	A. Cordero, Jr.
1975	Foolish Pleasure	J. Vasquez
1976	Bold Forbes	A. Cordero, Jr.
1977	Seattle Slew	J. Cruguet
1978	Affirmed	S. Cauthen
1979	Spectacular Bid	R. Franklin
1980	Genuine Risk	J. Vasquez
1981	Pleasant Colony	J. Velasquez
1982	Gato Del Sol	E. Delahoussaye
1983	Sunny's Halo	E. Delahoussaye
1984	Swale	L. Pincay, Jr.
1985	Spend a Buck	A. Cordero
1986	Ferdinand	W. Shoemaker
1987	Alysheba	C. McCarron
1988	Winning Colors	G. Stevens
1989	Sunday Silence	P. Valenzuela

PREAKNESS STAKES WINNERS

Year	Horse	Jockey
1873	Survivor	G. Barbee
1874	Culpepper	M. Donohue
1875	Tom Ochiltree	L. Hughes
1876	Shirley	G. Barbee
1877	Cloverbrook	C. Holloway
1878	Duke of Magenta	C. Holloway
1879	Harold	L. Hughes
1880	Grenada	L. Hughes
1881	Saunterer	W. Costello

Year	Horse	Jockey
1882	Vanguard	W. Costello
1883	Jacobus	G. Barbee
1884	Knight of Ellerslie	S.H. Fisher
1885	Tecumseh	J. McLaughlin
1886	The Bard	S.H. Fisher
1887	Dunboyne	W. Donohue
1888	Refund	F. Littlefield
1889	Buddhist	G. Anderson
1890	Montague	W. Martin
1894	Assignee	F. Taral
1895	Belmar	F. Taral
1896	Margrave	H. Griffin
1897	Paul Kauver	C. Thorpe
1898	Sly Fox	W. Simms
1899	Half Time	R. Clawson
1900	Hindus	H. Spencer
1901	The Parader	F. Landry
1902	Old England	L. Jackson
1903	Flocarline	W. Gannon
1904	Bryn Mawr	E. Hildebrand
1905	Cairngorm	W. Davis
1906	Whimsical	W. Miller
1907	Don Enrique	G. Mountain
1908	Royal Tourist	E. Dugan
1909	Effendi	W. Doyle
1910	Layminster	R. Estep
1911	Watervale	E. Dugan
1912	Colonel Holloway	C. Turner
1913	Buskin	J. Butwell
1914	Holiday	A. Schuttinger
1915	Rhine Maiden	D. Hoffman
1916	Damrosch	L. McAtee
1917	Kalitan	E. Haynes
1918	War Cloud (div. 1)	J. Loftus
	Jack Hare Jr. (div. 2)	C. Peak
1919	Sir Barton	J. Loftus
1920	Man o' War	C. Kummer
1921	Broomspun	F. Coltiletti
1922	Pillory	L. Morris
1923	Vigil	B. Marinelli

PREAKNESS STAKES WINNERS
(continued)

Year	Horse	Jockey
1924	Nellie Morse	J. Merimee
1925	Coventry	C. Kummer
1926	Display	J. Maiben
1927	Bostonian	A. Abel
1928	Victorian	R. Workman
1929	Dr. Freeland	L. Schaefer
1930	Gallant Fox	E. Sande
1931	Mate	G. Ellis
1932	Burgoo King	E. James
1933	Head Play	C. Kurtsinger
1934	High Quest	R. Jones
1935	Omaha	W. Saunders
1936	Bold Venture	G. Woolf
1937	War Admiral	C. Kurtsinger
1938	Dauber	M. Peters
1939	Challedon	G. Seabo
1940	Bimelech	F.A. Smith
1941	Whirlaway	E. Arcaro
1942	Alsab	B. James
1943	Count Fleet	J. Longden
1944	Pensive	C. McCreary
1945	Polynesian	W.D. Wright
1946	Assault	W. Mehrtens
1947	Faultless	D. Dodson
1948	Citation	E. Arcaro
1949	Capot	T. Atkinson
1950	Hill Prince	E. Arcaro
1951	Bold	E. Arcaro
1952	Blue Man	C. McCreary
1953	Native Dancer	E. Guerin
1954	Hasty Road	J. Adams
1955	Nashua	E. Arcaro
1956	Fabius	W. Hartack
1957	Bold Ruler	E. Arcaro
1958	Tim Tam	I. Valenzuela
1959	Royal Orbit	W. Harmatz
1960	Bally Ache	R. Ussery

Year	Horse	Jockey
1961	Carry Back	J. Sellers
1962	Greek Money	J. Rotz
1963	Candy Spots	W. Shoemaker
1964	Northern Dancer	W. Hartack
1965	Tom Rolfe	R. Turcotte
1966	Kauai King	D. Brumfield
1967	Damascus	W. Shoemaker
1968	Forward Pass	I. Valenzuela
1969	Majestic Prince	W. Hartack
1970	Personality	E. Belmonte
1971	Canonero II	G. Avila
1972	Bee Bee Bee	E. Nelson
1973	Secretariat	R. Turcotte
1974	Little Current	M. Rivera
1975	Master Derby	D. McHargue
1976	Elocutionist	J. Lively
1977	Seattle Slew	J. Cruguet
1978	Affirmed	S. Cauthen
1979	Spectacular Bid	R. Franklin
1980	Codex	A. Cordero, Jr.
1981	Pleasant Colony	J. Velasquez
1982	Aloma's Ruler	J. Kaenel
1983	Deputed Testamony	D. Miller
1984	Gate Dancer	A. Cordero, Jr.
1985	Tank's Prospect	P. Day
1986	Snow Chief	A. Solis
1987	Alysheba	C. McCarron
1988	Risen Star	E. Delahoussaye
1989	Sunday Silence	P. Valenzuela

BELMONT STAKES WINNERS

Year	Horse	Jockey
1867	Ruthless	J. Gilpatrick
1868	General Duke	R. Swim
1869	Fenian	C. Miller
1870	Kingfisher	E. Brown
1871	Harry Basset	W. Miller
1872	Joe Daniels	J. Rowe

BELMONT STAKES WINNERS
(continued)

Year	Horse	Jockey
1873	Springbok	J. Rowe
1874	Saxon	G. Barbee
1875	Calvin	R. Swim
1876	Algerine	W. Donohue
1877	Cloverbrook	C. Holloway
1878	Duke of Magenta	L. Hughes
1879	Spendthrift	S. Evans
1880	Grenada	L. Hughes
1881	Saunterer	T. Costello
1882	Forester	J. McLaughlin
1883	George Kinney	J. McLaughlin
1884	Panique	J. McLaughlin
1885	Tyrant	P. Duffy
1886	Inspector B.	J. McLaughlin
1887	Hanover	J. McLaughlin
1888	Sir Dixon	J. McLaughlin
1889	Eric	W. Hayward
1890	Burlington	S. Barnes
1891	Foxford	E. Garrison
1892	Patron	W. Hayward
1893	Comanche	W. Simms
1894	Henry of Navarre	W. Simms
1895	Belmar	F. Taral
1896	Hastings	H. Griffin
1897	Scottish Chieftain	J. Scherrer
1898	Bowling Brook	F. Littlefield
1899	Jean Bereaud	R.R. Clawson
1900	Ildrim	N. Turner
1901	Commando	H. Spencer
1902	Masterman	J. Bullman
1903	Africander	J. Bullman
1904	Delhi	G. Odom
1905	Tanya	E. Hildebrand
1906	Burgomaster	L. Lyne
1907	Peter Pan	G. Mountain
1908	Colin	J. Notter
1909	Joe Madden	E. Dugan

Year	Horse	Jockey
1910	Sweep	J. Butwell
1913	Prince Eugene	R. Troxler
1914	Luke McLuke	M. Buxton
1915	The Finn	G. Byrne
1916	Friar Rock	E. Haynes
1917	Hourless	J. Butwell
1918	Johren	F. Robinson
1919	Sir Barton	J. Loftus
1920	Man o' War	C. Kummer
1921	Grey Lag	E. Sande
1922	Pillory	C.H. Miller
1923	Zev	E. Sande
1924	Mad Play	E. Sande
1925	American Flag	A. Johnson
1926	Crusader	A. Johnson
1927	Chance Shot	E. Sande
1928	Vito	C. Kummer
1929	Blue Larkspur	M. Garner
1930	Gallant Fox	E. Sande
1931	Twenty Grand	C. Kurtsinger
1932	Faireno	T. Malley
1933	Hurryoff	M. Garner
1934	Peace Chance	W.D. Wright
1935	Omaha	W. Saunders
1936	Granville	J. Stout
1937	War Admiral	C. Kurtsinger
1938	Pasteurized	J. Stout
1939	Johnstown	J. Stout
1940	Bimelech	F.A. Smith
1941	Whirlaway	E. Arcaro
1942	Shut Out	E. Arcaro
1943	Count Fleet	J. Longden
1944	Bounding Home	G.L. Smith
1945	Pavot	E. Arcaro
1946	Assault	W. Mehrtens
1947	Phalanx	R. Donoso
1948	Citation	E. Arcaro
1949	Capot	T. Atkinson
1950	Middleground	W. Boland
1951	Counterpoint	D. Gorman

BELMONT STAKES WINNERS
(continued)

Year	Horse	Jockey
1952	One Count	E. Arcaro
1953	Native Dancer	E. Guerin
1954	High Gun	E. Guerin
1955	Nashua	E. Arcaro
1956	Needles	D. Erb
1957	Gallant Man	W. Shoemaker
1958	Cavan	P. Anderson
1959	Sword Dancer	W. Shoemaker
1960	Celtic Ash	W. Hartack
1961	Sherluck	B. Baeza
1962	Jaipur	W. Shoemaker
1963	Chateaugay	B. Baeza
1964	Quadrangle	M. Ycaza
1965	Hail to All	J. Sellers
1966	Amberoid	W. Boland
1967	Damascus	W. Shoemaker
1968	Stage Door Johnny	H. Gustines
1969	Arts and Letters	B. Baeza
1970	High Echelon	J. Rotz
1971	Pass Catcher	W. Blum
1972	Riva Ridge	R. Turcotte
1973	Secretariat	R. Turcotte
1974	Little Current	M. Rivera
1975	Avatar	W. Shoemaker
1976	Bold Forbes	A. Cordero, Jr.
1977	Seattle Slew	J. Cruguet
1978	Affirmed	S. Cauthen
1979	Coastal	R. Hernandez
1980	Temperence Hill	E. Maple
1981	Summing	G. Martens
1982	Conquistador Cielo	L. Pincay, Jr.
1983	Caveat	L. Pincay, Jr.
1984	Swale	L. Pincay, Jr.
1985	Crème Fraîche	E. Maple
1986	Danzig Connection	C. McCarron
1987	Bet Twice	C. Perret
1988	Risen Star	E. Delahoussaye
1989	Easy Goer	P. Day

TRIPLE TIARA WINNERS

(Formerly known as the New York Racing Association Filly Triple Crown, the Triple Tiara is made up of the Acorn, Mother Goose, and Coaching Club American Oaks.)

1968	Dark Mirage	1979	Davona Dale
1969	Shuvee	1985	Mom's Command
1974	Chris Evert	1989	Open Mind
1975	Ruffian		

BREEDERS' CUP RESULTS

Sprint *(6 furlongs)*

Year	Winner	Jockey	Margin
1984	Eillo	Craig Perret	nose
1985	Precisionist	Chris McCarron	$3/4$ length
1986	Smile	Jacinto Vasquez	$1^1/4$ lengths
1987	Very Subtle	Patrick Valenzuela	4 lengths
1988	Gulch	Angel Cordero, Jr.	$3/4$ length
1989	Dancing Spree	Angel Cordero, Jr.	neck

Juvenile Fillies
(1 mile, 1984, 1985, 1987;
1 $^1/_{16}$ miles, 1986, 1988, 1989)

Year	Horse	Jockey	Margin
1984	*Outstandingly	Walter Guerra	*
1985	Twilight Ridge	Jorge Velasquez	1 length
1986	Brave Raj	Patrick Valenzuela	$5^1/2$ lengths
1987	Epitome	Pat Day	nose
1988	Open Mind	Angel Cordero, Jr.	$1^3/4$ lengths
1989	Go for Wand	Randy Romero	$2^3/4$ lengths

* Fran's Valentine finished first by a half-length but was disqualified to 10th.

Mile
(1 mile on the turf)

Year	Horse	Jockey	Margin
1984	Royal Heroine	Fernando Toro	1$\frac{1}{2}$ lengths
1985	Cozzene	Walter Guerra	2$\frac{1}{4}$ lengths
1986	Last Tycoon	Yves Saint-Martin	head
1987	Miesque	Freddie Head	3$\frac{1}{2}$ lengths
1988	Miesque	Freddie Head	4 lengths
1989	Steinlen	José Santos	$\frac{3}{4}$ length

Distaff
(1$\frac{1}{4}$ miles, 1984-1987; 1$\frac{1}{8}$ miles, 1988-1989)

Year	Horse	Jockey	Margin
1984	Princess Rooney	Eddie Delahoussaye	7 lengths
1985	Life's Magic	Angel Cordero, Jr.	6$\frac{1}{4}$ lengths
1986	Lady's Secret	Pat Day	2$\frac{1}{2}$ lengths
1987	Sacahuista	Randy Romero	2$\frac{1}{4}$ lengths
1988	Personal Ensign	Randy Romero	nose
1989	Bayakoa	Laffit Pincay, Jr.	1$\frac{1}{2}$ lengths

Juvenile
(1 mile, 1984, 1985, 1987;
1$\frac{1}{16}$ miles, 1986, 1988, 1989)

Year	Horse	Jockey	Margin
1984	Chief's Crown	Don MacBeth	$\frac{3}{4}$ length
1985	Tasso	Laffit Pincay, Jr.	nose
1986	Capote	Laffit Pincay, Jr.	1$\frac{1}{4}$ lengths
1987	Success Express	José Santos	1$\frac{3}{4}$ lengths
1988	Is It True	Laffit Pincay, Jr.	1$\frac{1}{4}$ lengths
1989	Rhythm	Craig Perret	2 lengths

Turf

(1¹/₂ miles on the turf)

Year	Horse	Jockey	Margin
1984	Lashkari	Yves Saint-Martin	neck
1985	Pebbles	Pat Eddery	neck
1986	Manila	José Santos	neck
1987	Theatrical	Pat Day	¹/₂ length
1988	Great Communicator	Ray Sibille	¹/₂ length
1989	Prized	Eddie Delahoussaye	head

Classic

(1¹/₄ miles)

Year	Horse	Jockey	Margin
1984	Wild Again	Pat Day	head
1985	Proud Truth	Jorge Velasquez	head
1986	Skywalker	Laffit Pincay, Jr.	1¹/₄ lengths
1987	Ferdinand	Bill Shoemaker	nose
1988	Alysheba	Chris McCarron	¹/₂ length
1989	Sunday Silence	Chris McCarron	neck

Glossary

Across the board—A win, place, and show bet on a horse.

Added money—Money added by a racetrack to the amount paid by owners for nomination, eligibility, and starting fees.

All out—A horse extending himself as much as possible.

Allowance race—A race other than a claiming event for which the racing secretary drafts certain conditions.

Also-eligible—A horse officially entered in a race but not allowed to start unless the field is reduced below a specified number by scratches.

Also-ran—A horse who finishes out of the money.

Apprentice allowance—Weight concession given to apprentice jockeys. The allowance varies from state to state but is usually 5 pounds. A horse whose weight otherwise would be 119 pounds carries 114 if ridden by an apprentice.

Backside—The racetrack's barn area.

Backstretch—The straightaway on the far side of the racetrack. Also, barn area.

Bad actor—A fractious horse.

Bad doer—A horse with a poor appetite, a condition that may be due to nervousness or other causes.

Bandage—Strips of cloth wound around the lower part of a horse's legs, providing support or protection against injury.

Barrier—Starting gate, or a device used to start races.

Bat—Jockey's whip.

Bearing in (or out)—Deviating from a straight course. May be caused by weariness, infirmity, punishment, or simply the inability of the jockey to control his mount.

Bit—The metal bar placed in a horse's mouth for control and guidance.

Blanket finish—Horses finishing in such a close bunch that they could be covered by a blanket.

Bleeder—A horse hemorrhaging from his nostrils during or after a workout or race. The blood comes from a ruptured vein (or veins) in the nostrils, the pharynx, or the lungs.

Blind switch—This is a situation in which a horse is trapped between or behind horses and cannot pursue a free course.

Blinkers—Equipment used to limit a horse's vision and to prevent swerving from objects or other horses on either side of him.

Bottom—Stamina in a racehorse. Also, racing strip's sub-surface.

Breaking a horse—Getting a young horse accustomed to racing equipment and methods and carrying a rider.

Breakage—In the pari-mutuel form of wagering, racetracks pay off to a dime or a nickel, as required by state laws. If the breakage is to the dime, the bettor receives $2.20 on a horse who should pay $2.38. If breakage is to the nickel, the payoff on a $2.18 horse is $2.10. Generally, the breakage is split among the track, horsemen, and state or local municipalities in varying proportions.

Breakdown—When a racehorse suffers an injury; lameness.

Breather—Restraining a horse for a short distance in a race in order to conserve his strength or speed.

Breaking maiden—A horse or jockey scoring his or her first career win.

Bridge jumper—A big bettor who, if he loses, goes looking for a high bridge.

Bucked shins—An inflammation of the cannon bones. Confined for the most part to young horses, this ailment comes from horses with immature legs runnings on hard racetracks.

Bugboy—An apprentice rider (either male or female). The asterisk (*), resembling a bug, denotes an apprentice jockey.

Bull ring—A small racetrack.

Cast—This situation comes about when a horse gets in a such a position in his stall that he can't rise.

Chalk horse—The favorite in a race.

Chute—The extension of the backstretch or home-stretch to permit a straightaway run from the start.

Clubhouse turn—The turn at the point where the clubhouse is located, which is usually the bend of the track past the finish line.

Colors—Racing silks worn by jockeys to denote the ownership of a horse.

Cooling out—Restoring a horse to normal after he has become overheated from working out or racing.

Coupled—Two or more horses running in an entry.

Cuppy track—A racetrack with a surface that breaks under horses' hoofs.

Cushion—Surface of track.

Dead heat—Horses finishing on even terms.

Dogs—Low wooden portable rails positioned at a certain distance out from the rail on days when the track is muddy, to prevent horses who are working out from churning the footing close to the inner rail.

Driving—Strong urging by jockey.

Dwelt—Tardy in breaking from the starting gate.

Easily—A horse running or winning without being pressed by his jockey or by his opponents.

Entry—Two or more horses representing the same owner or trained by the same person and running together as a single betting entity.

Extended—A horse forced to run at his top speed.

Farrier—A horseshoer.

Flatten out—A horse flattens out when his head drops almost on a straight line with his body, a sign of exhaustion.

Fractional times—Intermediate times recorded in a race (quarter-mile, half-mile, three-quarters, etc.).

Freshening—To give a horse a rest after he has become jaded from racing or training.

Furlong—An eighth of a mile.

Girth—The band put around a horse's body to keep the saddle from slipping.

Green horse—A horse who acts and races erratically. A good many young horses are referred to as "green" because they lack racing experience.

Groom—A person who takes care of a horse in the stable. Also called a guinea or swipe.

Halter—The halter is like a bridle, except that it doesn't have a bit. It's used in handling horses when they're around the stable and not being ridden.

Hand—A four-inch unit used in measuring the height of horses from the withers to the ground.

Handicap—A race in which the handicapper assigns weights to be carried.

Handicapping—This is the study of factors in the past performances which determine the relative qualities and abilities of horses in a race.

Handily—Racing or working with moderate urging from the rider.

Hand ride—Urging a horse with the hands.

Hardboot—A Kentucky horseman.

Head of stretch—The beginning of the straight run home.

Homestretch—The front straightaway from the last turn to the finish.

Hung—A horse tiring but holding his position.

In hand—A horse running under moderate control with speed in reserve at the call of his rider.

In lily whites—A horse with his legs wrapped in white bandages.

Irons—Stirrups.

Juvenile—Two-year-old horse.

Leaky roof circuit—Minor racetracks.

Length—The length of a horse from his nose to tail—eight or nine feet.

Lug—When a horse attempts to bear in or out.

Maiden—A horse that hasn't won a flat race in any country.

Maiden race—An event for non-winners.

Mudder—A horse who runs his best on a muddy or soft racing surface.

Mutuel field—Starters running together as a single betting entity. These starters are considered to have the smallest chance of winning.

Near side—The left side of a horse, which is the side he's mounted on.

Oaks—Stakes race for 3-year-old fillies.

Odds-on—A price less than even money.

Off side—The right side of a horse.

Off track—A track that is not fast.

Off-track betting—Legal betting permitted at a betting parlor or at a racetrack other than the track where the race is run.

On the bit—A horse who is eager to run.

Osselets—Arthritis of the fetlock joint, causing enlargement of the ankle.

Overland—Taking a horse to the outside and around his opponents.

Overweight—Extra weight carried by a horse when a jockey isn't able to make the required weight. This is limited to not more than 5 pounds.

Paddock—Structure or area where horses are saddled and kept before going to the track.

Paddock judge—The official in charge of the paddock and the saddling routine.

Pasteboard track—A racing strip that is light-ning fast.

Patrol judge—Officials who observe the race from various locations around the track.

Pinched back—A horse in tight quarters and forced back.

Placing judge—Official who determines the or-der of finish in a race.

Post parade—Horses going from the paddock to the starting gate.

Quarter pole—The pole a quarter of a mile from the finish.

Racing secretary—An official who drafts the con-ditions for the races.

Rogue—A bad-tempered horse.

Route horse—A horse who can race long dis-tances.

Savage—A horse biting another horse.

Short horse—A horse not trained up to the last ounce of his energy and thus not fit enough for the race he's running in. He'll tire, and his stride will shorten before the end of the race.

Silks—Jacket and cap worn by jockeys.

Sophomores—Three-year-olds, connoting second season in racing.

Splint—A small bony enlargement between the splint bone and the cannon bone.

Stale—A horse off form.

Stewards—The top officials at a race meeting.

Stick—A jockey's whip.

Stretch turn—The bend of the track into the home-stretch.

Sulk—A description applied to a horse who refuses to extend himself.

Tongue strap—A strap or tape bandage used to tie down a horse's tongue to prevent it from choking him in a race or workout.

Under wraps—A horse under stout control in a race or workout.

Walkover—A race which winds up with just one starter, who is required by the rules of racing to merely gallop the required distance.

Washy—A horse who becomes so nervous that he sweats profusely before a race.

Breeding Terms

Blue Hen—A broodmare who is a prolific producer of top horses.

Bottom line—Thoroughbred's breeding on the female, or distaff, side.

Breeder—Owner of dam at the time that foal is born.

Bred—A horse is bred at the place where he is foaled. Also the mating of horses. If a horse is conceived in one state and foaled in another, he is listed as being bred in the latter. For example, Lady's Secret, the 1986 Horse of the Year, was conceived at Claiborne Farm, near Paris, Kentucky, but she was Oklahoma-bred because that's the state where she was born.

Broodmare—A mare who has produced a foal.

Dam—Mother of a thoroughbred.

Foal—Newly born thoroughbred (male or female), or until weaned.

Inbreeding—Duplication of the same name or names in a pedigree.

Mare—A female horse who is 5 and up.

Matron—A mare becomes a matron when she has been covered by a stallion.

Prepotency—The capacity of a sire or mare to transmit his or her character and physical characteristics to his or her get.

Ridgling—A male horse with an undescended testicle.

Sire—A horse (5 years and over) becomes a sire when one of his get wins a race.

Stallion (or Stud)—A horse becomes a stallion once he has been retired and bred to a mare.

Top line—Thoroughbred's breeding on the sire's side.

CREDITS

Pages 5–9 Copyright © 1990 by News America Publications Inc. Reprinted with permission of the copyright owner.

Page 11 Courtesy of Arlington International Racecourse.

Page 12 Courtesy of Ladbroke DRC.

Page 30 Courtesy of Ladbroke DRC.

Page 34 Courtesy of Ladbroke DRC.

Page 67 Copyright © 1990 by News America Publications Inc. Reprinted with permission of the copyright owner.

Index